D1449315

PRAISE FOR
Happiness is Running
Through the Streets to Find You

"Bruno's fine book describes the experience of recovering from trauma and transforming pain into love and joy. This deeply empathic book will inspire and guide others as they make the same journey."

⌒ **Mary Pipher, PhD,** Author, *Reviving Ophelia*
and *Women Rowing North*

"Holly is indeed translating trauma's harsh legacy into healing – for herself but also for the reader. In the Head Start community, we know Holly to be an energizing and engaging voice as a trainer and advocate, and while reading her story is at times heartbreaking, her hopeful and triumphant energy shines through. Holly artfully intertwines her personal reflections with sage advice and scientific research that draw you into both her personal journey and the broader conversation surrounding childhood trauma. You will come away from reading feeling eternally grateful for Holly's vulnerability. It will no doubt inspire countless others to tell their own stories and embrace their own strength."

⌒ **Yasmina Vinci,** Executive Director,
National Head Start Association

"Robert Staub writes that there are seven acts of courage that one must commit in order to live an authentic, purposeful life. He says that the seventh act is the courage to act—to put oneself on the line, in harm's way. In Holly Bruno's memoir, she has definitely committed the seventh act by publicly speaking her truth and her pain. Her narrative inspires us to reflect, and challenges us to confront our own pain and trauma in order to be a better person—and by extension, a better caretaker of the children and families we serve."

Maurice Sykes, Author, *Doing the Right Thing for Children: Eight Qualities of Leadership*

"Holly Elissa Bruno has done it again! In her latest work, Holly has carefully and sensitively balanced the emotional minefield of trauma with the healing words of stories that flow with deep understanding, direction, and comfort. While personal trauma may seem unsurmountable, Holly guides with care, juxtapositions, and the ahas! of self-reflection and discovery. Each bite-size story or anecdote takes the reader on a personal journey in the healing process. This excellent format lets the reader follow a direct approach or simply pick any story or 'chapter' at random. And each will certainly lead to unexpected personal reflections, with the option to return later for extra good counsel. The topics will challenge, fire old hurts, produce tears, and ultimately provide peaceful joy. Thanks to Holly for the courage to bring this work forward!"

Luis A. Hernandez, ECE Specialist
TTAS/Western Kentucky University

"*Happiness Is Running Through the Streets to Find You* is a remarkable book, written by a remarkable woman. When I think of how easily Holly Elissa laughs and loves, given everything she's endured, I am in awe. To say that her story is a testament to the human spirit is to use a cliché, but there's simply no other way to put it. Because of Holly Elissa's courage in writing this book, readers will have a much greater understanding of and empathy for children who have experienced trauma."

Rae Pica, Author, *What If Everybody Understood Child Development?*

"In her memoir *Happiness Is Running Through the Streets*, Holly Elissa Bruno tells a story of recovery from trauma, that is both particular and universal, using poetic language to intuitively navigate the layers of family legacy and political context. Her narrative is not linear, but clear and easily followed. The connecting thread is always healing, as she follows her inner compass that no matter the despair, never seems to quite break. And the courage required to follow that path toward spiritual wholeness should inspire others to do the same in their own lives. Bruno's message is that nothing is irreparable, no damage so great that healing cannot undo. Bruno has lived the adage that as long as there is life, there is hope. And in a world that has been so very traumatized by exploitation and ignorance, that is a message that applies to us all."

Stacia Tolman, Author, *The Spaces Between Us*

"What a departure from Holly's previous books, was my first thought. After reading it I realized it's the pinnacle of her writings and a must read for leaders. Whether you've endured trauma firsthand or not, Holly's words give hope to survivors and a point of empathy to supporters. Simon Sinek says, 'empathy is the most important instrument in a leader's toolbox.' The honesty in Holly's story is enlightening, thought provoking and inspiring. Holly's life embodies 'that which does not kill us makes us stronger.' And in the truest Holly spirit she leaves us with her mantra, 'Why not laugh? The alternative is despair.' "

⸻ *Vernon H. Mason, Jr. M.Ed.*
Author, Humorist, Keynote Speaker, Workshop Trainer

"I am honored to have had the opportunity to read Dr. Bruno's very personal perspectives and head, heart and soul of her growing, developing and moving from a tragic past to a remarkable present and wonderful future. I felt the anger, frustration, terror, wonder and remarkable resilience and developmental journey that has brought Holly to where she is today, a remarkable educator, speaker and champion. I appreciated the personal views, experiences and history, and yet, I was also astounded by the 'Q&A' and therapeutic conversations that can take place in her book. As an educator, professor, and former children's mental health professional, I found her honesty, her courage and ability to see humor, strength and courage out of a past that should not have been, remarkable. Bravo Dr. Bruno!"

⸻ *William H. Strader,* Professor,
Early Childhood Education Coordinator,
New England Symposium on Play

"It takes a strong person to face what has happened to you and to come out stronger and to tell about it. We never know what a child is going through at home so we help them the best we can."

*— **Barbara O'Neal,** Director,*
Muscogee (Creek) Nation, Office of Child Care

"There's a reason why Holly is in great demand as speaker and colleague. In a world of 'talking points,' she delivers 'straight talk.' Her honesty and generous spirit leaves me inspired and hopeful."

*— **Valora Washington,** Chief Executive Officer,*
Council for Professional Recognition

"Holly Elissa Bruno tells her story in a way that is unique but will be relatable to so many survivors of childhood trauma. She speaks of finding resources within herself and the natural world to help her survive inescapable experiences. She describes her complex path to not only managing her pain, but also healing from it. Her story is sure to be validating and inspiring to others who have been through severe trauma and are on their own path to healing."

*— **Ricky Greenwald, PsyD,** Founder and Executive Director,*
Trauma Institute & Child Trauma Institute, and Author,
Child Trauma Handbook and *EMDR Within a
Phase Model of Trauma-Informed Treatment*

Happiness is Running Through the Streets to Find You

Translating Trauma's Harsh Legacy into Healing

Holly Elissa Bruno

Exchange
Press

ISBN 978-0-942702-46-0

Printed in the United States by Sheridan.

© Dimensions Educational Research Foundation, 2020

Book design by Stacy Hawthorne with Kaitlyn Nelsen.
Illustrations by Abigail Ervin-Penner. Editing by Sara Gilliam.

For more information about other Exchange Press publications and resources for directors and teachers, contact:

Exchange Press
7700 A Street
Lincoln, NE 68510
(800) 221-2864 • ExchangePress.com

Dedication

To all children and adult children enduring
a love deficit, may my story offer hope:
We always deserve love;
we never deserve abuse.

Ever since happiness heard your name,
it has been running through the streets
trying to find you.

—⁊—

Hafiz

Table of Contents

I Marvel

*If you want to know where to find
your contribution to the world, look
at your wounds. When you learn how
to heal them, teach others.*

~σ~

Emily Maroutian

I marvel at folk who know the shape of their lives from early on.

High school classmates in the early 1960s recited the exact number of children they would birth, the floorplan of their marital home, a job description for the person they planned to marry.

When they asked how many children I planned to have, I responded, "Three sounds good."

I made that up. I never envisioned getting married. Frothy white wedding cake gowns were not my dream. I looked over the hilltops surrounding Corning, New York, and reminded myself: *My life begins over those hills.* I couldn't see beyond the hills, but I knew my life beckoned from the other side.

My dream?

Freedom.

I came to this earth a spunky, playful, adventuresome child. I was not going to give that up.

The life plan of law school classmates whose fathers were attorneys was to join the family law firm and eventually take over.

Murphy and son, Clifford and son.

Bruno and daughter? I didn't see that sign over anyone's office door.

I didn't know I could be an attorney. In 1973, as I leapt boldly naive into the promise of the law, I discovered only three percent of American attorneys were women, people of color or both. Without Atticus Finch and Perry Mason, I would have had no clue what lawyers do. Word of Ruth Bader Ginsberg had not reached me.

So much I did not know. So much I dreamed of a shimmeringly meaningful and fulfilling future. So much I yearned to reshape my cobbled-together self into a person who could leave her world a bit better. Daily, I slipped clothing on over a body stuck together with band-aids of denial, rubber bands of dissociation, stale bubble gum of grandiosity and in-your-face determination.

I used acceptable drugs (work addiction adrenaline, achievement endorphins) and available self-medication (disappearing through dissociation) to survive, while avoiding or hiding addictions that would bring shame upon my family ("demon" rum, free-wheeling sex, self-abuse). I sassily strutted the runway of our "perfect family" fashion show, following last after our Grace Kelly mother, stalwart father, and my two high-achiever older sisters.

We three "Bruner girls" accumulated advanced degrees like Girl Scout badges:

- PhD (2)
- MD (1)
- JD (2)
- MA (1)
- MS (2)

One sister confessed, "I only felt loved when I was getting a degree." I had no vision of a life outside a school or university campus. So, I kept going to school.

If I wasn't over-working and over-achieving, I feared knee-capping anxiety or shame attacks would fell me. I couldn't handle depression. So, I ran. Diagnoses such as panic disorder and complex post-traumatic stress disorder didn't exist. I figured I was crazy like the women in my family. But that was a secret I could never tell.

If I witnessed an event my father didn't approve of, he would correct me: "You didn't see that, daughter."

The real war is at home.

Bessel van der Kolk

Fumes of my embalmed past choked me willy-nilly. I begged suffocating nightmares to dissipate in a firecracker's poof. I willed phobias—triggered by heights, tunnels, guns, spiders and family gatherings—to scatter from me like termites from a collapsed wall.

Safety was both an illusion and the promised land. "Feeling out of control, survivors of trauma often begin to fear that they are damaged to the core and beyond redemption" (van der Kolk, *The Body Keeps the Score*). I ran outside to the forest to fill my lungs with the scent of crushed mint, even in frigid midwinter. In nature, I revived; in my father's house, I, struggled to survive.

Mine is an everywoman's story, a #MeToo memoir.

We who experience trauma's harshness prefer we had not. Oblivion, through denial or other forceful obliteration of the truth, is the alternative to facing our harsh legacy. Oblivion eradicates searing pain that won't quit.

The problem is oblivion, like alcohol, holds us hostage, keeps us stuck on its flypaper of lies. Here's the truth I was programed to hide. I am:

- a trauma survivor
- an incest survivor
- an abuse and neglect survivor
- a survivor of violence
- living with complex (from repeated abuse) PTSD and depression
- fighting for freedom to live and breathe freely

For most of my days (and nights) I could not trust my own voice or believe my story. My birth family didn't just keep secrets, they enforced lies. Convinced the tsunami of truth inside me would drown me if I opened my floodgates, I avoided remembering what I knew to be true.

The price of walking out of the fog of oblivion is high. Family members once part of my heart turned their backs. Parents who birthed me disowned me. My mother was so ashamed of me, she wouldn't speak of me at her prayer group no matter how much she missed me.

Banished from our packs, lone wolves don't live long. Without our pack to support and defend us, we are at the mercy of strangers. In my case, strangers have become the family I dreamed I would have.

Happiness finds me when I find myself, as I strip off the Puritan hair shirt that dug into my skin. Happiness finds me hatching out of the all-elbows Rube Goldberg contraption I erected to survive. Happiness, having run through the streets all my life to find me, embraces me when I choose to stop running.

My story is true for me. It's how I make sense of my experience. To family members who experienced our past differently, *namaste.* I speak only for myself. We each have our own memories and inter-pretations of events. I have included no living person's name without permission and, when appropriate, I have created pseudonyms. This is a personal memoir, not a factual family history. My recollection may not be accurate in every detail; however, my story is real as this morning's sunrise. As a poem reveals deeper truth than a newscast, and a myth more meaning than a ship's log, I offer my story of hope.

I share my story to claim my survivor's birthright to joy.

If you join me on this adventure, you may discover you also want to seek out, honor and believe your untold story. May you find hope that lights the night sky and clarity you never believed could be yours.

No One Steals my Soul Anymore

Nothing on this earth or in the heavenly realms can overwhelm or overcome you when you know who you truly are.

Mooji

Plans collapse when trauma comes unbidden as an avalanche, unwanted as a car crash, unforeseen as a gunshot. Trauma creeps in stealthily, repetitiously, and silently as nighttime intimate violation of a child, or daytime demeaning of a child's worth:

"You ought to be ashamed of yourself. Can't you do anything right? What do I have, pigs for daughters?"

Avalanche, car crash, gun shot or behind-closed-doors violation can define us and predetermine the trajectory of our lives. The Adverse Childhood Experiences study predicts years will be hacked off our lives by childhood trauma, and names illnesses likely to fell us—stroke, heart disease, addiction. Burgeoning research in brain development foretells lasting brain damage if children do not experience healthy opportunities and loving support between ages zero and three.

Every time I read these death sentences I want to bellow, "Stop! That is not the only story, not the only result. Stop pronouncing us doomed! Witness our resilience. Trauma faced has become our spiritual guide home."

Trauma is deadly, yes, to body and spirit. Wounded people die from gunshots, suicide, addictions, extreme choices and broken hearts.

Trauma does not have to kill the soul. No one steals my soul anymore. On that I have made my choice.

Trauma can be something other than a neck-breaking albatross. Trauma is my most rigorous guide. Trauma is my unchosen but compelling pathway to a life of meaning, an uplifting appreciation of beauty and a deeply anchored conviction to make the world better for every child.

Our painful past can become our greatest asset if we choose. Declaring a truce with trauma has given me my life back. Without that truce, my life was stolen, buried with my ancestors' histories.

Learning from trauma, even admitting we were traumatized or that our lives have not been as seamless as they appear, is difficult. Trauma slashes hope and poisons dreams. Trauma's acid dissolves smiles and erodes confidence.

I write this book to claim trauma as my teacher. Trauma and I are intimate. We are not BFFs, but together we know what makes me tick. If I don't let trauma kill me, trauma is my ladder to healing. I befriend my traumatic experiences to grow in authenticity. Paradoxically, my vulnerability becomes my greatest strength. Trauma's shame grenades no longer inflict soul death; their threat is my wake-up call to choose courage.

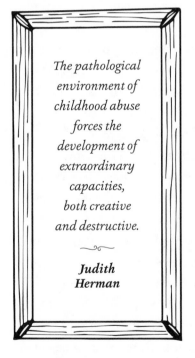

The pathological environment of childhood abuse forces the development of extraordinary capacities, both creative and destructive.

Judith Herman

I cannot learn from this exacting guide without asking for help, without learning to trust, without opening my heart to love unfettered. I cannot recover without forgiving myself for being traumatized, which means I must forgive my abusers while holding them accountable for the abuse. I forgive myself for not being able to save them from their demons. As a fellow survivor said of his perpetrators, "I can't get sick enough to make them well."

You know a traumatized person. Or several. You may be one. Trauma can terrorize at any age. Surgery is trauma. Loss is trauma. Trauma is an abrupt, life-stopping moment of being threatened with extinction. That trauma locks us in its prison.

This book is the unfolding truth of a feisty child who unevenly raised herself, quirkily taught herself to think and never forgot how to laugh. This book is the story of the adult who despite honors and accomplishments could not feel at home in her own body or stop driving herself. This book tells of my desire to rejoin the human race, not set myself falsely above others or throw myself under anyone's bus.

Walk with me as I share my story? I will be at once gentle and honest by telling my truth with love. I have learned to let go of resentment or the misplaced need to even the score. I am no longer in a power struggle with my perpetrators. I have come to understand they did to me what was done to them. Just as I did to my children things for which I needed to make amends. The person I hated most was *me*.

I write this book for every trauma survivor who seeks freedom from the kamikaze self-abuse sword handed to us with our first commandment: Thou shalt not love thyself.

In the manner of trauma survivors, I share floating vignettes from my childhood. We trauma survivors have a "cover story," a quick way of signaling what happened without evoking pain of the events. Our stories don't emerge with traditional "beginnings, middles and ends," because our brains don't remember that way. Memories float in and out, called out by triggers rather than conscious command.

Only when we are truly heard can we speak. Only when we speak, can we believe ourselves. Only then, feeling safer from threat of annihilation, can we climb out of our cover story.

Trauma is boot camp for our own brand of intelligence, if not wisdom. Listen to Maya Angelou, Oprah Winfrey, Elie Wiesel, Nelson Mandela, or Pema Chödrön to hear trauma's poetic prophecy.

I take heart from the poet Hafiz who calls to us to notice where we are: "I can see angels sitting on your ears, polishing trumpets, replacing lute strings, stretching new skins on the drums, and gathering wood for the evening's fire. They all danced last night, but you did not hear them."

Listen. Hear yourself and hear your guides. Walk beside me through the streets? We don't have to run. Happiness is patient and devoted to finding us.

PART I
Learning the Drill

We cut over the fields at the back with him between us—straight as the crow flies—through hedge and ditch.

~∽~

Charles Dickens, Oliver Twist

Late winter evening with dear friends Jack and Nina, Mildred, Ingrid and Brian. Dinner at Nona Lucia's Tavola, where gnocchi float like cumulus clouds in sauces that pique toward perfection. Playful conversations, self-effacing laughter, authenticity, an evening easy on the heart.

At the intimate recital afterwards, pianist Victor Rosenbaum performs late Brahms, Beethoven, Schubert, with poignancy. Each piece was composed within close range of the artist's death. Rosenbaum wistfully reminisces, "Schubert walked one mile to a lesson on counterpoint in his final week on earth." In his final year, Schubert was 31.

Hope cannot fail a seeker's heart.

After Rosenbaum's final bow, we amble about Kalliroscope Gallery in Groton, Massachusetts, lush with Henri Matisse, Marc Chagall and Paul Matisse creations. Comfortably we explore, talking of the music, our lives and our work.

She with the Ph.D., Nina's friend Dr. T. begins to describe her efforts with orphaned, traumatized babies. Heart open, I listen. I know traumatized babies. I, too, want them to be comforted, loved, and soothed on their long path toward healing. I thank the doctor for her dedicated work, affirming that the early years are crucial for a child's development. We talk of brain development and social-emotional development. Agreements cavort like Schubert's trout.

It is then that Dr. T. speaks that word: *irreparable.*

"If we don't get to these children early, the damage is *irreparable.*"

My mind twists up like a circling crow. Un-repairable. Damaged. Doomed. Disabled. The person irreparably damaged can never be made whole. Unsalvageable. All the king's horses and all the king's men cannot put a broken child together again.

Circling crow lands on my shoulder nudging me to speak.

I hear my voice, my strongest, clearest and most direct voice respond, "I invite you not to use irreparable when speaking of traumatized children. If that child experiences a loving relationship at any point in her life, she can heal. Her process is more difficult and painstaking; however, she can heal. We cannot rob a child of hope."

Nina intervenes. "Resilience. Some children have remarkable resilience. We have talked about that." Nina's words sooth us both. The paintings re-engage our imaginations.

Let us praise remarkable resilience.

Let us honor hope.

Let us trust healing is possible.

Without hope, traumatized children self-medicate to make it through days and nights. Oblivion calls through substances like beer, OxyContin, sugar and processes like overwork, driving ourselves to perfection. When we self-medicate, we eradicate ourselves.

DO CROWS FLY IN A STRAIGHT LINE?
'As the crow flies' is a pretty common saying but it isn't particularly accurate. Crows do not swoop in the air like swallows or starlings, but they often circle above their nests. Crows do conspicuously fly alone across open country, but neither crows nor bees (as in beeline) fly in particularly straight lines. Before modern navigational messages were introduced, crows were kept upon ships and released when land was sought.
Crows instinctively fly toward land.
⌢ **BBC Science Focus Magazine**

Stories unfolding tell themselves. Your story and mine unfold soulfully when we trust we are being heard. Until we find our listener(s), our witness, our stories encapsulate in hiding places. All we see of the turtle is his shell.

Circling is natural to a crow. But when she's exiled at sea and senses land, our crow, released, flies straight toward land. She is flying home. A trauma survivor's soul, like our determined crow, knows the way home even if we do not.

FINDING OUR WAY HOME

We seek to find our way home with instincts clear as the crow's. A survivor's resistance to homecoming is equally hard wired: "I will be washed away by a tsunami of tears. If I allow myself to cry, I will never be able to stop." I have discovered my terror of not being able to breathe is interlaced cruelly with dread of expressing anger long hidden.

Was I suffocated for crying? I recall swallowing my tears, gulping them down my throat, a Hobson's choice: silence or annihilation. When children are not helped to process trauma, we survive by cobbling together our own pathways.

We pretend we are not bleeding out.

Milagros tells me her overwhelmed mother threw a fork at Milagros that landed quivering like an arrow in her calf. Which pain is worse? Not crying from the wound or exposing family abuse to a doctor? Children learn to lie. We lie to ourselves.

She didn't mean to hurt me.

Put it behind me.

Forget about it.

We fool ourselves into believing we are happy when our hearts ache. We settle for half a life. If we don't wake up to this harsh love deficit, we come to the end of our lives "only to discover that we have not lived" (Thoreau).

Most of us avoid conflict because conflict retraumatizes us. Ruptures tear the heart. We bleed again. Reminders of shame or abandonment rip the skin off our deepest grief. Our hidden unhealed wounds are exposed. Milagros's pierced leg heals; she walks as if nothing happened. She wonders:

Did it happen?

My mother loves me.

My mother wouldn't hurt me.

The broken heart weeps without tears, closing up like a clam each time a stone is thrown.

UNEXPECTED PASSAGEWAYS

Crows circle unless they must find their way home. When the sea separates them from their home on land, "crows instinctively fly toward land." Our heart's desire to find our way home can drive us down unexpected passageways.

I did not believe I could handle this unexpected passageway. This passage felt counterintuitive, opposed to lessons I had learned about survival. To find my way home, I had to turn toward pain.

The conflict that hurts so? Crack it open to find the gem: your purpose, what matters to you.

I had mastered the art of avoidance. Painful memories were taboo, off limits, dangerous to be recalled. By avoiding pain, I was not living.

Now I know to sit with pain, breathe through the hurt, not run.

My blood red recliner facing the fireplace serves as my mourning hammock. In this sanctuary, I choose, when craziness (of grief, pain, terror, disorientation) comes, to allow it to come, witness it, feel it. I feel it.

When I can, I weep for it. Shame, like a gestapo marches through me: "You have betrayed your family by feeling." I sit until I hear shame goosestep away. When the gestapo is far enough away, I release myself. Weary, I sleep. My body keeps a new score.

My pain is familiar, as familiar as my running. One snowy winter afternoon, I did not run. I wept for the unloved, unseen, unwanted baby girl. My exposed heart at last released her agony. "It's never too late to have a happy childhood" (Wayne Dwyer) sounded like a lie until that moment.

Even if they're a crowd of sorrows, who violently sweep your house empty of its furniture, still treat each guest honorably. He may be clearing you out for some new delight.

— Rumi

Hopelessness is an illusion, a gripping force, but an illusion. I can choose to be an actor not a reactor. In time, in the fullness of time, confidence grows. "The last of the human freedoms is to choose one's attitude in any given set of circumstances," observed psychiatrist, Viktor Frankl in Auschwitz.

Like a crow, I am flying over deep waters to find home.

DIVINE DESPAIR

Even years later traumatized people often have enormous difficulty telling other people what happened to them. Their bodies experience terror, rage, and helplessness, as well as the impulse to fight or flee, but these feelings are almost impossible to articulate. Trauma by nature drives us to the edge of comprehension, cutting us off from language based on common experience or an imaginable past.

*⁓ **Bessel van der Kolk,** The Body Keeps the Score*

Words, the heart's power to articulate experience, saved me even as my voice was beaten out of me.

I memorized poetry, words that sang in my heart. Words that sang to my soul. Words that comforted me. I never recited the poems out loud to anyone. I archived the words within my heart for dark times when I needed to call upon their magic.

I memorized this Tennyson poem from a Sunday New York Times Book Review after church. Sundays were a day of rest. No chores. No yelling. No human connection in that house except through written word.

> *Tears, idle tears*
> *I know not what they mean.*
> *Tears from the depths of some divine despair,*
> *Rise in the heart and gather to the eyes.*
> *In looking at the happy autumn-fields and*
> *thinking of the days that are no more.*
> ⁓ **Alfred, Lord Tennyson**

Tennyson's words rise in my heart each New England autumn when I walk through golden meadows, past the pond at Louise Doyle's estate, and think of red-winged blackbirds migrating south to a warmer, more welcoming winter home. Every autumn, I miss them.

Music spoke to my soul even more poignantly than poetry. My father's record collection of heavy black grooved LPs was sacred: Stravinsky, Rachmaninoff, Tchaikovsky, Grieg, Bizet, the Mills Brothers. My sister and I would listen, making our separate sense out of "The Firebird," "Peer Gynt," "Boléro."

Once I heard "Swan Lake" on the radio. I was enraptured; my heart memorized each note. One summer morning, Mrs. Stebbins was driving me to the pool with her two sons. "Swan Lake" came on the car radio. I sighed, "Swan Lake," before I could silence myself.

Surprised, Mrs. Stebbins asked, "It is 'Swan Lake', but how do you recognize it so quickly?"

Quickly I covered myself: "Oh, I've heard it lots of times," I lied. Bruner girls were not allowed to call attention to ourselves by standing out. Bruner girls were required to have brains, beauty and personality while believing we had none of these.

"Swan Lake" and I lifted off together, the dance playing secretly inside me.

When my big sister was crowned queen of the junior prom, I bounded toward her, bubbling with joy for her, wanting to congratulate her. My parents intercepted me and spun me around: "Don't say anything to her," they scowled, "It will go to her head."

STAY BACK, EVIL DEMONS

I worked myself up, pulled open the cellar door, flipped on the light switch that shone down the wooden stairs. Loudly, authoritatively as a five-year-old could be, I commanded the demons down there they had better not bother me.

I am brave, I warned.

I am tough, I pronounced.

I am not afraid of you, I spouted.

You stay right where you are. Don't even think of tromping up these stairs, I postured.

I had been left in the dark house by myself. I preferred being alone to being with the tribe. But the house itself clutched dark secrets. Demons that lurked at night, hovering in dark hallways, must have lived somewhere down there.

The cellar floor was coffee-brown dirt, damp enough to grow mushrooms. Only pale light filtered through dirty cellar windows. The windows were horizontal rectangles placed beneath the earth, which was held back from them by an aluminum window well in which I would place hop toads I befriended.

That cellar was my father's domain of machinery he tended like the furnace, the water softener. His jagged saws, his wooden handled hammers, his axe and his hatchet, his nails and his screwdrivers, his paint brushes and tarps and turpentine, and his All Things Male, dominated and defined that dark place. My mother would yell he needed to finish it off.

"When are you going to cement the cellar floor?" she yelled every Saturday, chore day.

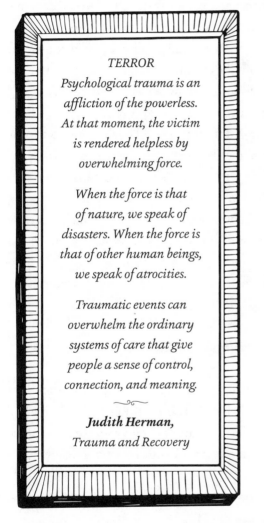

TERROR

Psychological trauma is an affliction of the powerless. At that moment, the victim is rendered helpless by overwhelming force.

When the force is that of nature, we speak of disasters. When the force is that of other human beings, we speak of atrocities.

Traumatic events can overwhelm the ordinary systems of care that give people a sense of control, connection, and meaning.

Judith Herman,
Trauma and Recovery

He never finished the cellar floor while we were children, only after we had left his house. The dark cellar was his domain.

There writhed demons of my nightmares.

I pretended to myself and to the demons that I would not allow them up the stairs. They could not come into the light, those creatures of darkness. Before I took my commanding stance, all four feet of me, I scanned my trajectory to the front door and then to the back door. I reassured myself if dragon or demon swelled up at me, I would outwit them by running out the door into the yard. I had confidence in my speed. I was fleet of foot. That protection I had honed.

Posturing invincibility helped me pump up adrenalin to fight rather than to flee. But, fight or flight teetered beyond my control as I attempted to command the dark powers before they could overtake me.

Grandiosity, this is called. Grandiosity is the enlarged view children project of ourselves onto dangerous tableaus. If I could be an actor, not a reactor. If I could become larger and stronger like a sparrow puffing out her feathers or a squirrel plastering its fluffed-up tail behind its head to extend its height, I might survive.

I desperately needed to believe I had the largeness of spirit to survive.

The child is the father of the man.
*⌒ **William Wordsworth***

I have carried this practice of grandiosity into my adulthood, or perhaps the little girl that still lives inside me, whom I call "Hollywog," has held tight to this practice. She and I align when we act as if we know what we are doing, step up to take on challenges we are not at all sure we can handle.

In 2008 as I struggled to write my first book, *Leading on Purpose*, I got a call from my publisher at McGraw-Hill.

Can you finish the book by March?

I gulped. Swallowed. June had been my goal.

Okay, if you need it by March, I can do that. You mean end of March, right?

No, we need it by the beginning of March to meet our new publication schedule.

The five-year-old girl at the top of the cellar stairs whispered in my ear: *Just say yes.*

Yes, I can do that.

I did that when I had no idea I could.

That was a textbook, innovative for sure in its theme of emotional intelligence and its direct conversation with the reader. But, at the same time, "Leading on Purpose" was safely shored up by ample research, Daniel Goleman's insights, and accepted organizational development theory.

As I write this book, my feisty inner child Hollywog and I battle through our disbelief that we can complete such a skinless book. If we can force or cajole ourselves to sit down at the desk, we write nonetheless. We write until we can believe in ourselves by clicking "Word Count" and surprising ourselves with page count.

Typing, I fear I may betray my parents' memory, provoke my extended family members by breaking the silence, and face exile again.

A book is flimsy as a bubble on a pond until it is finished and published. Truth telling is exhausting when what was true was struck down as a lie. To survive, I had to obey my father's command: "You didn't see that, daughter." What I had seen with my own eyes could not be trusted.

ENTERING THE MADNESS

My mother named all our cats except one, which my father named Cougar for his elongated, sleek Siamese cat body. Posy was our first cat when we lived in Nellie Scully's first floor apartment on "Irish Hill," where outside my window the drunken man would stumblingly sing his way home most nights.

Madness began in that apartment. Or more accurately, that is where I entered into the madness. The madness had been passed down for generations, if not centuries. When a family harbors mental illness, the family is tainted. *Omerta* or *malocchio*, the evil eye, forever curses and resides in family members.

My grandfather, Michele, (pronounced Mick Kelly), could flash the admonishing eye. He was ruling patriarch of his immigrant family. Grandfather Michele never spoke to me. I could skip unnoticed down Lime Street in Rochester, New York's Sicilian ghetto as my father Vincenzo Bruno and grandfather Michele walked to Modello's corner market to pick up freshly stuffed cannoli. The men spoke words that floated up from the sidewalk like music, echoing another continent. Their words sang with vowels, dancing in my ears. They spoke their language, Italian with a Sicilian dialect.

Michele was my father's model for manhood. My father barely spoke of his father. When I asked my centenarian father on one of those long afternoons in the stale air of the house where I had been raised, "What was your father like?", my father responded with surprising candor.

"I've been thinking about that. He was too strict."

I breathed in and breathed out, looking through the picture window from my chair in the living room, waiting until my next question could be stated matter-of-factly, revealing no neediness.

"Can you tell me what you mean by saying your father was too strict?"

"I felt his hand on my rump too often," Vincenzo Bruno responded. Then he closed up. Closed his eyes and began to snore.

My father was admitting his father spanked him too much, yes. My father was owning that his father hit him often. That was revealing in itself.

Was my father also admitting he was abused sexually? Men in that family had a pattern of abusing daughters physically and in my case, sexually. No one talked about that pattern directly, but, some of us lived through it and others just knew. The practice had passed on to the next generation as it had perhaps been handed down to my grandfather's generation. Did patriarchs sexually abuse sons too?

I have no evidence that men abused men sexually. Yes, children were beaten, screamed at, had their hair pulled, ears pulled, were thrown against walls, told they were nothing. My male cousins, a few of them, have told me this much. One cousin, now long dead, told me all he remembered of his childhood was being beaten. Screamed at and beaten.

Was there more? Sexual abuse no one will own. So, I shall own mine because otherwise secrets kill. Otherwise, holding down the atrocity, I rupture inside.

THE CAT, THE HATCHET, THE CURSE
Nothing ever goes away until it has
taught us what we need to know.
⌒ Pema Chödrön

One family cat Timothy, a grey and white tiger, was a "mouser," roaming meadows, catching mice. Timothy was a house cat by day, resting from his night shift. I was little and knew nothing of proper hugs or how to treat beings smaller than myself. I do not recall being hugged or held.

I liked to feel Timothy's fur on my skin. Hugging him close, I did not know to gather his hind legs up with one hand beneath. One morning, alone outside by the meadow, I picked Timothy up and hugged him, leaving his hind legs dangling. I liked his purring warmth and the protective feel of his fur. The moment was sweet as the meadow breeze.

Timothy had enough. Perhaps he sensed a mouse nearby or grew tired of being confined.

Signaling his urge to be free, Timothy scratched my face just underneath my left eye, unleashing blood. My father emerging from the house, spying blood, shifted into slow motion deliberateness. His eyes riveted me. I had learned early to stand still, not move, to become invisible while fear drained color out of me. Invisibility could keep me out of harm's way.

Deliberately, my father strode back into the house, down into the basement where he kept his tools. A moment later he emerged with his hatchet in hand. Again, peering straight into my eyes, my father turned, and then took off after Timothy to kill the cat with the hatchet.

Timothy was fast in the way of cats. Fast and savvy at survival. Far faster than I, even though I had learned to run fast to survive. Unable to catch his prey, my father walked, hatchet held stiffly by its neck, back down to the cellar.

If Timothy had died, I would be the cause. If I hadn't hugged him so closely, he wouldn't have scratched me nor would my father have flamed violent. I froze into a pillar of salt in the yard, unable to move. Aware I had caused my father's rage, almost caused Timothy to be hatcheted, I could not live with myself.

This was my father's house. He controlled my world. I could not stop him to save the cat without putting myself in the way of harm. Shame riveted me silent. I would not speak for decades about this.

When adults' actions make no sense to children, children make sense of impossibility by blaming themselves. Judith Herman observes, "Violence or murder threats may also be directed against pets; many survivors describe being forced to witness the sadistic abuse of animals." Because that trusting, furry kitten's vulnerability was so close to my own vulnerability as a child, I feared for my life.

Finding themselves as the cause of bad things, needing to believe adults protect us, children cannot admit to ourselves that adults harm us. I got the message: I was, to quote Jonathan Edwards, "a sinner in the hands of an angry God."

DENIAL AS A WAY OF LIFE

Years later, I participated in my first Incest Survivors Anonymous meeting at the Meadows Recovery Center in Wickenburg, Arizona. Although most of us were women, men sat in the circle too. There, I witnessed our common belief: *These people we trusted could not have violated us. It couldn't have happened. They were supposed to keep us safe from harm.*

We knew the truth; yet, we couldn't make room inside ourselves for it.

When cats are wounded, their skin closes quickly, covering the wound before it heals. A toxic abscess swells beneath the fur. The cat must be taken to the vet to have the abscess lanced. Otherwise, the cat might not survive.

Telling these stories feels sharp like lancing my heart. Each lancing opens room inside me for the truth.

Was it possible my father wanted to kill the cat for the harm it had caused me? I never felt that. My father provided four walls, food and heat. My father could not love me from the moment I betrayed him at my birth.

HOUDINI BABY

A man, a tall force towers darkly over my sister's bed across the room. I am afraid to witness, to breathe. I try to squeeze my body like Houdini through the wooden slats of my crib so I can melt into the wall and escape.

Sleeping is never safe. I don't sleep deeply until dawn.

I am choking. I gasp. I cannot breathe. I am terrified to swallow. Tonight, he comes to my side of the room. To my crib. Forcing my baby hands. My baby mouth. Forcing so harshly, so unbearably, I abandon my body. I picture myself climbing out the window over the roof into the starry night.

Jacob's golden ladder has come for me.

Individual Reflection Questions

1. Did you ever pretend to be someone else, braver than you were, or "act as if you were fine," when you felt anything but strong, safe or fine? In those moments, did you believe in yourself and feel you were powerful? What helped you get over this posturing? Or, do you find yourself still posturing to protect yourself in unsafe situations or with difficult people?

2. How do children instantly know who's in charge? What non-verbal signals do adults give off to let children know who is in power? Can you think of benevolent ways in which adults let children know who is in charge? Hurtful ways?

3. How did reading the author's childhood experiences affect you? Were you surprised, or in any way reminded of your own experiences as a child? Would you have behaved differently in those circumstances? Have you memorized poetry, quotes or songs to call upon when you need their comfort?

Book Group
Discussion Questions

1. Does your family hold to the directive, "Don't air our dirty linen in public"? Were you raised—or did you raise your children—to keep family "business" in the family? What is the reason for that privacy? What are the effects, both beneficial and detrimental, of keeping family secrets?

2. Incest is for many a taboo topic. Why is that? How could we talk about this pervasive issue more openly? What resources are available to families to get help with this generationally passed-on behavior? What leads to incest?

3. Trauma is a major public health issue, according to Judith Herman. Why don't we treat and prevent trauma within families more aggressively? What would help change attitudes to render trauma more discussable and preventable?

PART 2
In Youth, it Was a Way I Had

In youth, it was a way I had,
To do my best to please.
And change, with every passing lad
To suit his theories.
But now I know the things I know and do the things I do.
And if you do not like me so,
To hell, my love, with you.

~⟳~

Dorothy Parker

SAFE OUTSIDE

I learned to keep secrets, hide, become invisible. I learned to please people who could hurt me. I learned to live two lives: inside and outside.

Inside my father's house I was prey. I hid in different places. In the off-limits-to-children living room, I condensed like an embryo behind the overstuffed chair. I scooted beneath the second-floor eves in the darkness where adults could not fit. The cats had discovered that hiding place too and pooped there. Holding my breath was necessary.

Outside I was free. I would wake in the early morning, make myself a peanut butter and jelly sandwich on Wonder bread, fill an army canteen with water and silently walk out the side door. A benefit of being neglected was no one noticed my absence. As long as I crossed the door at dinner time, I could roam all day. I felt safe in the woods and the high meadows. In the fanciful way of children, I felt protected.

Inside I crouched. Outside I ran free. Outside was home.

One frosty autumn morning, I determined to run away, get to town, board a bus south. Hiding in the foot well of the black Ford's backseat, I waited for someone to drive to town. I trusted I would not be noticed or missed. Cold, damp, cramped and hungry, I gave up and walked back inside because I had to pee.

FIRST CHOSEN FAMILY

I dreamt I was being raised by gray wolves with electric lemon eyes in the opalescent moon glow on the high meadows of Spencer Hill, safely up above the coursing Chemung River. Rivers flood in Spring. Children leaping and teetering from ice floe to ice floe can be sucked down river. I felt safe with wolves and their knowing eyes. I longed to warm myself in the gray fur of their underbellies. Wolves were my imaginary friends.

As untended children do, I befriended animals while clambering up and down hillsides, seeking pollywogs, blackberries and hickory nuts in season. Wilhelmina, a neighbor's soft, dear and slobbering Saint Bernard lumbered down every day to see me. She was my height and I hugged her neck and buried my face in her fur. She even let me try to ride her like a pony. Her softness and loving brown eyes made my heart ache. If wolves were my imaginary friends, Willie was my true friend.

One day, the next day and the day after, my Wilhelmina didn't lumber by. I missed her so, I asked my mother where Willie was.

She had been killed because a prissy neighborhood girl said Willie bit her.

"Willie's head was sent to Cornell Veterinarian School to check for rabies."

My Wilhelmina? Rabies? Never. Sweet Willie never bit anyone. But no one asked me.

My sweet Wilhelmina, decapitated, just as Timothy almost was.

My heart could not bear my longing for my friend.

One year, my photo appeared in a *Corning Leader* line-up of public-school summer camp children showing off our animals. Holding high in my right hand my unnamed "pet," a lazy, willing garden snake I picked up from a driveway while walking to South Corning Elementary School, I posed with left-hand-on-hip attitude beside children holding dogs' leashes and squirming kittens in arms.

Snake and I parted shortly after the photographs were snapped. Our time was brief; but we were family in those moments. Did I say *thank you, Snake?* I do now. *Thank you, Snake, for allowing me to belong in the line of photographable elementary school children.*

I was four in October of 1950, drawn to a long-fallen tree trunk rotting like tuna fish dumped from a can in the morning rain.

As I dug into the soft dampness with my hands, of a sudden, the right cuff of my red and black checked woolen jacket swelled with bustling movement. I was delighted. Curious, not afraid. I was safe in my woods. The small furry force tramped up to my shoulder, padded round my neck, zipped down my left sleeve and exited my left cuff, a star-nosed mole whose domain I had entered.

A star-nosed mole. Wilhelmina. Snake. Wolves. These brothers and sisters I trusted.

MY OLD OAK TREE

She stood sentinel over the Chemung River valley. Stood proud and tall and elegant in the architectural way of trees. Welcoming me. Spreading powerful arms open wide. Anchored in a century of unseen deep roots. Anchored prior to the Civil War. Secure alongside the Underground Railroad to Canada. Sentinel for hope. Brave sentinel growing straight up from a twenty-degree hillside.

I leave the house without notice, again served by my gift of invisibility. My mother screamed if the screen door slammed shut: "Pigs for daughters! Pigs for daughters! What do I have, pigs for daughters?" Silent, I was unseen. My soul ached to soar. Soaring was possible only outside the house on Orchard Drive.

To hike the hillside to my friend, Old Oak Tree, I begin my two-block trek to the dead end of Orchard Drive, past the Dershams, the O'Learys, Charlie Chase's, the Johnsons, the childless couple's home, the Reillys, Gottkos and Marne Gray's fenced "estate" where Frog Pond begins. Peepers chortle, courting spring just beyond the spongy damp of thick moss clumps.

I stop to watch darting pollywogs as they break free of gelatinous egg sacks hung like bunches of translucent grapes under water. In just-birthed wonder they dart, these pollywogs, ecstatically claiming movement. I witness legs develop, tails diminish, bodies stretch lanky and green. Pollywogs, nascent frogs, fascinate me. I squat observing.

Early morning cold nudges me to say goodbye to the 'wogs. I climb the meandering thin path through straw-like hollow reeds, through dried stands of last season's goldenrod, past my trove of winter berries, stopping to taste a crimson wintergreen berry that smacks of mint. I watch hawks patrolling and listen for the sound of clear water flowing. Was this an old well? Someone's meadow spring? Water so clear I cup my hands to drink it in. Water so clear I taste heaven.

Through copses of birch then pines. Beech then a blueberry barren, small and protected. Up the hill. Up the hill until I could look up to see her. My home. My beloved tree. My sacred perch above the valley, far enough beyond houses to be safe, far enough beyond my mother's scream, I find sanctuary.

Who was the person who hung the primitive swing of log suspended on thickly braided wire cable? Who cared so for the souls of children? Who so loved us to foresee our hearts' desire? I never discovered his name or his decade; but how I loved his swing! How I loved his swing that lifted me to heaven.

Heavy the log and rough the cable. I gathered the log close to my chest to haul the swing, which was suspended straight down from a high branch on my Old Oak Tree. I was not afraid to place my left foot on the left side of the log and cable and jump on, so that my right leg straddled the cable. Down, down, then up over the valley I glided until heaven scooped me up above the valley, until no one could hurt me. No one could trap me again. No one could beat me, enter me, try to annihilate me. No one. No one could harm me in the arms of the Old Oak Tree.

Chemung River glistened below as if diamonds were strewn over it like skipping stones. The hawks and I flew. I was safe.

Crows landed and rested on the Old Oak Tree's branches.

BLACKBERRY GATHERER

Come August, I claimed the dented aluminum colander from beneath the drawers in my mother's Formica kitchen. Up the hill I trekked again, climbing further to my secret troves of the most onyx of all, sweetest of all blackberry thickets. Only honey bees and I knew how to find such holy places. Only we watched and waited as green berries became white became red became black then that deepest of indigo purple.

What one loves in childhood stays in the heart forever.

Jean-Jacques Rousseau

In silent respect, I plucked each blackberry and dropped it into the colander to hear its sweet trumpeting ping. Ping. Ping until my fingers were stained, my belly was full and honey bees no longer envied my smile.

Honeybees did not sting me and I did not fan them away. We understood our work.

Colander brimming, pride in my balanced steps, back down from my secret garden I clambered until I reached the well to bless my hands. Cold water refreshing my mouth, cooling my forehead and un-sizzling my thick, dark hair. Down the hill, past birch copses, blueberry trove, the frog pond, down the street until I found a sweet un-yelling mother like Ruth Dersham who would always bake a blackberry pie with me. White sugar sprinkled on the blackest of berries. Crisco crust. Dots of butter. Kool-Aid tastes great while we wait.

Vanilla ice cream dripping on top. Pie à la mode. My heart and belly warmed. My heart and belly full.

No one told. We all kept our secrets. Silence had merit. The women knew. They baked pies with me. They did not question me or mention my mother.

I WAS OKAY ENOUGH, UNTIL...

Until my pals in the 'hood, Janie, Billy, and Phyllis announced at the end of summer, they would be first graders. Me too, I assumed. We were pals, more family than my family, daily companions. Janie, Billy and Phyllis and their moms had all marched down the hill and taken the "cut-through" behind neighbors houses to red brick South Corning Elementary School with its liberty bell on the roof outside the second floor.

When I told my mother we needed to register too, she said I was not allowed. Not allowed to be with my friends? What difference did it make that my friends were already five!

My New Year's Eve birthday both disqualified me from first grade and would dump me in the just founded half-day kindergarten with the littles. I wasn't having any of it. I didn't care that I was four. I was a grown up! What would I do without my buddies? I could do everything Janie, Billy and Phyllis could, and sometimes more.

Children feel intense rejection when they are exiled from their peers. I was going to school and that was that! I was using up one of my three wishes. I couldn't admit to myself or to anyone else why I had to go to school. Becoming a first grader was non-negotiable. School would be my safe haven.

I took my mother by her hand and walked to the school, requesting to speak with the person who had made the wrong decision. Busy Mrs. Bebout (rhymes with shout-out) grudgingly admitted my mother and me to her office. She scowled while announcing her time was limited. What was this about?

My mother sat in a chair against the office wall, quiet as a church mouse (I never understood that saying; I could hear mice scurry) while I stood straight and intent.

Mrs. Bebout, I am ready to go to first grade.

Your record says you will not be five by October 1. No, you cannot. Anything else?

Mrs. Bebout, my friends Billy, Janie, and Phyllis are all going to first grade. I want to be with my friends.

No, they have already had their fifth birthdays.

Mrs. Bebout, I can do everything Billy, Janie, and Phyllis can do. Sometimes I do things faster.

That doesn't matter. You fail to meet the requirement.

Mrs. Bebout, I know I am ready for school. I want to learn.

My four-year-old self argued my case, persisting until the impatient principal—who was assuredly not my pal—grudgingly threatened, "Look here! I'll give you six weeks to prove yourself. If you can't keep up, I don't want to see you in this school until next year. Am I clear?"

"Yes, thank you, Mrs. Bebout, you are clear," I replied, backing out the door.

There was a rightness in her decision. I felt that. My path cleared from the underbrush. I had spun fear into advocacy. I would be okay. I would *keep up.*

I would be free.

My greatest wish had come true: Freedom unfurled as my enduring dream.

As a child, my job was to raise myself and get through the day. I didn't have guidance and my role models were arbitrary and authoritarian. No one asked, "What do you think?" As a result, I did the best I could to figure out how to think and how the world worked.

I did not trust authority figures, and from early on was "authority counter-dependent," opposed to giving respect to someone because s/he held a position of power.

Similarly, I learned to rely on myself and not expect help from anyone. I set high standards for myself to master tasks, skills and situations. When I succeeded, I felt safe. If I did not succeed, I felt ashamed and scared, because failing left me vulnerable. Being vulnerable with animals was fine. Being vulnerable with people was dangerous.

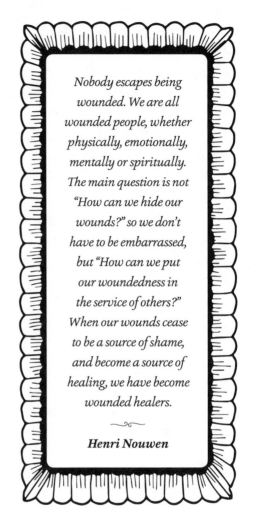

Nobody escapes being wounded. We are all wounded people, whether physically, emotionally, mentally or spiritually. The main question is not "How can we hide our wounds?" so we don't have to be embarrassed, but "How can we put our woundedness in the service of others?" When our wounds cease to be a source of shame, and become a source of healing, we have become wounded healers.

Henri Nouwen

Traits of Children of Alcoholic/Dysfunctional Homes

1. *We became isolated and afraid of people and authority figures.*
2. *We became approval seekers and lost our identity in the process.*
3. *We are frightened by angry people and any personal criticism.*

⌒ **Tony A.,** *The Laundry List*

Later on, I would learn that these traits I developed (distrust of authorities, "people pleasing" those who could hurt me, fear of criticism) are shared by survivors of childhood trauma. In addition to the first three traits of *The Laundry List*, I also excelled at trait 12: "We are dependent personalities who are terrified of abandonment and will do anything to hold onto a relationship, in order not to experience painful abandonment feelings which we received from living with sick people who were never there emotionally for us."

My "love deficit" began on that New Year's Eve when I was born, the year hydrogen bombs exploded in Hiroshima and Nagasaki to end Hitler's war.

Individual Reflection Questions

~⁊~

1. Where was your "safe place" as a child, that one place where you felt totally at home, protected, free from danger of any sort? As an adult, have you found ways to replicate that safe place?

2. Did anyone frighten you as a child? If so, how did you act when that person was near? Did you find ways, like the author, to hide? Did you attempt to please the scary person to win her favor and diffuse the danger? As an adult has your way of behaving around difficult/dangerous people changed, or do you still avoid or "people please"?

3. What do you recall about first starting school? How were you introduced to the school, your teacher, your classmates? What helps children adjust to school and their classroom? What do you imagine the author's first day of school was like, given her experience with principal Bebout and the rules?

Book Group
Discussion Questions

1. How important is being outdoors "in the wild" to children? What can children learn in nature that is harder to pick up in the classroom? How do changes in our natural environment (bees becoming endangered, loss of songbirds and fireflies, weather changes due to global warming) affect the life lessons children learn today by being in nature?

2. How valuable are animals to humans? What do children (and adults) learn from taking care of pets? Have pets been an important part of your life? What do you think about schools having therapy dogs in the buildings to comfort children (and staff)?

3. When children intuitively proclaim, "That's not fair," what might their definition of fairness be if they could articulate it? What was the definition of fairness that Principal Bebout attempted to enforce? What was fair to four-year-old Hollywog? Have you noticed other times when opposing definitions of fairness have caused conflict?

PART 3
Desperately Seeking the Divine

I came to the earth with a belief in goodness, a trust in human kindness.

Perhaps that's why I felt especially raw to human cruelty. I felt so at home in the presence of kind people that I could not bear to lose them. In second grade, I asked my fun-loving gym teachers, Mr. and Mrs. Georgen, "May I please go home with you?"

Every Christmas, I would imagine trudging through snow until I found the home of a childless couple who were thrilled to take me in as their gift.

When my parents came to collect me after a summer living in the Allegheny Mountains with my cousins, I asked to stay in Knapp Creek instead. Aunt Janet's buckwheat pancakes were slathered with melting butter and homemade maple syrup and I never felt in danger sharing my cousin's room.

I had been farmed out to the underpopulated mountains to escape the polio epidemic that killed my best friend in first grade, Claire. Claire's death shook me and set me on a quest to understand why bad things happen to good people. Believing innately as I did in the goodness in people, I urgently sought out a home where love endured.

Raised by an evangelical, born-again Baptist mother and Sicilian Catholic father, I was warned about evil sinners. In contrast to hell, I liked the sound of heaven. Angels could fly, blow trumpets and watch over little children. Above the clouds, angels lived in a soft pastel, beautiful beyond description heaven. Heaven sounded like home to me. In my young mind, I reasoned: Why not find heaven now?

This quest for the divine would stay with me all the days of my life. I am not religious, but I am spiritual, in that I have always sought a life of deeper meaning based in love. Part of my spirituality is my heart's desire to connect with the divine, the transcendent, the great spirit healer I could not see, but trusted I would be able to feel.

I experienced memorable adventures seeking that heaven where love abounded and cruelty was unknown.

DIGGING FOR JACOB'S LADDER

We Brunos did not hold family meetings or group decision-making sessions or gather in circles for conversation. We did sit still and bow our heads as my father said grace at the dinner table before every meal. We sat straight and ladylike as he read Bible stories in the living room. Those stories were as age-appropriate for a three-year-old as Edgar Allen Poe's "Masque of the Red Death!" No matter how hard I squinted to concentrate, I quivered with questions I was not allowed to ask.

I managed to ask at church, however, where I could find Jacob's glimmering gold ladder to climb up to heaven. I was ready to climb up to angels who would patiently listen to me, play harps, talk with me and help me understand why my friend Claire died. Maybe Claire was waiting for me there!

A church lady advised I could find Jacob's ladder of gold if I looked hard enough and believed deeply enough.

I commenced digging. Too small to heft a shovel, I dug with a gardening trowel. Our cellar's dirt floor was common in homes built in the 1940s and earlier. I dug up the cellar floor in abiding hope I would unearth Jacob's ladder. If I worked hard enough and dug long enough, my trowel would strike a solid golden rung. And when I found the ladder, no matter how weary I was, I surely would climb to heaven. Life would be a dream, a bowl of cherries, ripe with delirious happiness.

I always restored the earthen cellar floor, tamping down the just-freed earth with my trowel. Why compound disappointment with punishment?

Holy Rollers were a religious sect in the southern tier of New York state. I was taken by their name, the Holy Rollers, and had to know more. No one could tell me much more than assumptions.

"They must roll around the floor to get religion" was the best anyone could conjure. I wanted to know if that worked. Could I roll my way to heaven? I hatched another plan. The First United Methodist Episcopalian Church's sanctuary was shaped like an amphitheater, sloping down to the altar. When my mother, a devoted church lady long before Saturday Night Live immortalized her clan, took me to church, I planned to roll my way to heaven.

The church sanctuary sported teal carpet aisles, which carved lines straight down through the semi-circling rows of pews to where the preacher spoke; and behind the preacher, the choir sang. That sanctuary presented a perfect set-up for me to employ my new skill: the forward roll.

Our elementary school didn't have a gym for gym classes. Instead, itinerant teachers, Mr. and Mrs. Goergen, would come to our classroom to offer "physical education." We must have practiced rolling between our desks, in the cloakroom at the back of the classroom, or even at the front of the room in the teacher's lair around her thick oak desk. The Goergens showed us how to roll: clutch your knees, tuck your head and rock forward. Or did we rock forward and then clutch our knees? Whatever the drill was, I got it and I loved it. I was a natural, *bona fide* forward-roller.

Confident in my forward-rolling skills and called to those blue-green sloping carpets, I readied myself at the back of the sanctuary, which I had to myself one late weekday afternoon.

I grabbed my knees, tucked my head, rocked back first, rocked forward next and leaned into my accelerating spin down the aisle.

Okay, I bumped into a carved pew early on, but I righted myself to begin again: Clutch knees. Tuck head. Rock back. Rock forward. I rolled and rolled toward the Divine, envisioning gleaming pearly gates winging open for me while angels sang.

"Jesus loves the little children, all the children of the world."

Fare thee well, Veil of Tears. I was going to get me some love!

Jacob's ladder couldn't save me. Holy Rollers must have been on something, because, I crashed into the wooden pillars that surrounded the preacher's lair. Bang! Instead of enlightenment, a clunk at the altar.

SIGN ME UP FOR A NEW LIFE

When my Brownie Scout troop in our chocolate milk-colored uniforms marched single file into the community church for a revival preacher, we heard that preacher promise with resounding emphasis: we would be born again if we dedicated our lives to our lord and savior, Jesus Christ.

I elbowed Janie.

"Let's do it! Don't you want a new life?"

Janie's Catholic self was reluctant, but I persuaded her to step up to the altar beside me. I couldn't wait for the sky to open and my life to sparkle with sunbeams. Preacher lady whispered something into each child's ear. When she got to Janie and me, I leaned forward eagerly.

"Meet me in the choir room," she said.

"Oh, man, we gotta wait, Janie! Don't give up. Something will happen in that next room."

We waited atwitter. All that happened was preacher lady asked us to forsake our wicked ways and follow the commandments. Of course, we agreed. I looked to the ceiling: angels mine, where are you!

I concluded that finding Jacob's ladder, rolling to the pearly gates, and being born again were not what they were billed to be. Why didn't adults tell the truth?

Probably because the truth spelled trouble. When my Sunday school teacher was reading about Nicodemus (Nick who?) being born again, I raised my hand. Curious, I asked for an explanation, a description.

"Do we get born again by climbing back inside our mothers and coming out again?"

The red-faced (I didn't get why) teacher pointed springer spaniel-rigid to the doorway and commanded me out to stand in the hallway. I didn't get that either. I wanted to know how things work. How do people get born, again?

I learned the anxious humming of the classroom when a student is expelled. Each subsequent time I would hear that sound it buzzed louder. In that moment, I was relieved not to have to sit and hear about old Nick-oh-dee-moose. Maybe he was just an ig-nor-aye-moose. All those pale dour born-again relatives I had? They never seemed happy anyway. I resolved to find another way to the Promised Land.

A TALENT FOR SETTING THINGS FREE

Bolts of lightning crack the sky in half. Rain gods beat timpani drums calling me. No time to waste. These portentous moments pass as they come: boom. Gone.

Pulling up my ratty, puckered blue nylon swimsuit, I bolt out the front door. Once again, neglect has benefits: no one is paying attention to me. In glee, I slide across the slickened grass. Twirl in the downpour. Play hide and seek with myself between sheets of rain. Giggle at my freedom. Slide down a slippery grassy knoll. No one but I would be out in this enchanting downpour.

It's a little girl's pony ride of an afternoon.

Down from Spencer Hill rush rivulets of raindrops, sluicing now toward the Chemung River. Freedom! Freedom calls. Yippee, let's wash home to the sea.

I know my purpose. I was meant to do this. I rush to the ditch where my parents' front yard abuts the cindered and tarred street. Torrents of water overflow the ditch, blocked with twigs and rocks and chunks of cement from builders' discards.

I set about my work unblocking. I rid the water of impediment after impediment, one branch after another, one cement chunk or discarded broken brick after another. I un-wedge them, pry them loose, throw *impedimenta* to the side. Water flows deeper, faster, gushing now. I work my way down the hill, freeing the chute to the exuberant flow.

No one sees me. No one knows. No one cares.

I feel me. I know. I care. This removing of obstacles. This freeing of forces. This opening wide to the flow. This is what I do. This is what I am meant to do. This is my gift.

I stand, appreciating my work. Splashing through the torrents in awe. I see myself swimming to the river to swim to the sea. I remembered my pencil sketch of the wooden raft I would nail together from discarded lumber to sail down the Chemung river to freedom. I mused too of my sketch of the earth house my friend Janie and I could live in like sisters if we slapped walls of mud pies together on the hillside by our Old Oak Tree.

Feeling safe and accomplished, I stand alone dripping on the painted red cement front porch, trying to shake off the water like Wilhelmina would have shaken her wet coat.

I have become adept at silently opening and closing doors, finding my way, floating around obstacles into a room where I can dress without being noticed. Joy in my soul. I have claimed me my little girl's pony ride of an afternoon.

RITE OF SPRING: MY MOTHER'S ANNUAL CARTWHEEL

Mother would walk out the back door from the dining room, hefting a basket of clean damp clothing on her hip like she might heft a child.

My job was to reach into the basket, shake out and hand up one item at a time for her to hang on the white rubber-encased clothesline that joined together an apple tree and a beech tree in the backyard. We used wooden clothespins that turned from beige to gray with the seasons.

Once each spring on a supremely cloudless day, I waited for my mother to emerge with the day's laundry so I could begin my service. *Please, mother. Just once mother. You can do it, mother.* She refused over and over, dismissing me with a wave of her free hand.

Each year the charm of my hopefulness cast its spell. *Please mother, do your cartwheel. Do it for me. I love your cartwheels.* A childlike smile bloomed out of my troubled mother's hidden inner place.

She stepped off the cement porch, put the basket down, raising her right knee, leaned precipitously forward, landing on one hand then another hand, her legs whirling. She landed on her feet! She performed her cartwheel.

Once every spring. My mother's cartwheel just for me. Making my mother happy made me happy. I knew we were ok. God was in God's heaven. All was right in that world.

UNSUNG MOTHER MINE

My sisters did not share these moments of light with our mother. They identified with our father, idealized him as their "rock."

Years later, I knew to move my father's photograph so my sister Karen could see it as she lay dying. At her memorial service, Karen's church folk said, "Karen never mentioned your mother. She spoke so glowingly of your father."

Only as an adult did I come to understand that abusers become saints in the eyes of the abused. That cloak of many colors we clothe our abusers in disguises and prettifies unbearable reality. When I participated in that incest survivors' group, we all wedged together into the paradox.

"My family member abused me. But it couldn't have happened. He was my father, my uncle, my grandpa. He couldn't have done that."

We knew; but, our knowing was too painful to bear.

CURIOUSER

When I heard characters in books being granted "three wishes," I longed to be asked what my three wishes were. I puzzled over the question, 'What do I most desire?' To seek gold or beauty and castles would have quickly turned sour. Lesson learned: Things could not guarantee happiness. I weighed asking to live forever until I realized that wish would also spell unhappiness when friends died.

At last my answer came clear: ask for as many wishes as I want. That way, I could forever be happy, forever able to ask and to receive what I most desired. My fallback was to ask for wisdom. With wisdom, I would be at peace.

Girded with my answers, I hankered to be asked, "What are your three wishes, child?"

Like Jacob's ladder, no wish granter appeared; so, I pursued my quest down other paths. No holy rolling to Heaven's door. No endless wishes. I determined to discover the Divine in other ways.

THE DAY MY SOUL FLEW TO ITS SAFE HOME
Anyone who has suffered a trauma knows, first, paralyzing fright, followed by the bereft feeling of losing your way in the world, of being severed from your very soul.
⁓ Peter Levine

Some gifts come without fanfare. An insight is carried on a breeze. An unlikely angel hovers over to protect. Help desperately needed arrives just in time.

These are gifts of healing. Bouquets left at my doorstep. Open the door, Hollywog, to see what awaits you.

As I slid down the wall to the linoleum floor, I watched it fly away, that point of light in a moving arc. I watched it separate from my heart, lift above and soar away. I watched my soul leave my pounded body. I watched my soul find its way home to safety when my world went black from pounding fists.

For the longest time after that beating, I felt halved. I ached for the part of myself that had to flee. I was angry too. This is not right, this being a lost soul.

THE BODY FINDS ITS OWN WAY TO GOODNESS

I lost my soul at age fourteen late one afternoon. Back home after the school day, I cleaned house for my mother. "Having a nervous breakdown" we couldn't talk about, my mother primarily holed up on the second floor of the house. She had lost weight and wore black instead of her signature lipstick pink.

"Traumatized people are fragmented and disembodied," Peter Levine observes.

She appeared at the top of the stairs spewing thunder bolts down at me.

"Can't you get anything right? What is wrong with you? What do I have, pigs for daughters?"

Why couldn't I make those hardwood stairs sparkle? Why had I missed a speck of dust?

The thing is, the stairs sparkled. Dust was 800 percent banished.

Her Saturday yelling sessions had bled their way into any day.

Today, her wrath was focused on me alone. My sisters had gone off to college, one after another. My mother had no minions to command but me. Her spirit was so ruptured, she had to pour her fully brimming outrage onto me. I fought back the insanity transfer. I cleaned. I scrubbed. I vacuumed the same spot. My mind took its white glove to every inch of the stairs. My inner ears blazed red with the searing shaming of her screams.

Hearing my father open the back door as he returned from work, a mad woman posing as my Mother threw me under his bus.

"Look at that, Jim. Your daughter can't get anything right! Look at those stairs. Look right there. See where she missed that spot?"

There was no spot. He knew that. He consulted with me late each afternoon before he entered the house, expecting a report on her current state. He didn't want to step ungirded into her wildly fluctuating weather systems.

He and I would walk outside, side by side, as I reported my observations of her day. I clasped my hands behind my back out of respect for my work, respect for the sacredness of caregiving, like a research scientist, summarizing behavioral trends and moods.

She's calmer today.

She's anxious today.

But on this day, I had had enough. I said it. Not knowing my honesty would bury me alive for years, I told the truth. I thought he would understand. He had heard my reports. He had counted on them and on me. We were colleagues of a sort, weren't we? I could trust our bond as keepers of this family secret? I had felt closer to my father in those meetings. We served together on the same smoky battlefield.

"She's crazy," I told him. Hadn't he appointed me her caregiver, her nurse, her cook, her cleaner, her cheerleader?

Ah, the depth of my mistake. I said, "She's crazy." The truth that could not be denied could never be spoken.

Out of the blue, he punched me. Threw me against the wall, smacked me, pounded me down the hallway into the back room, pounded and pounded and pounded me into the coffin-like built-in plywood cabinet he had created to store the vacuum cleaner. Just before I slid to the floor unconscious, I watched an undaunted point of light rise from my heart and lift silently off in its slow arc to safety. To survive, my soul abandoned my body to fly to a place free of violence.

Murderous rage is deadly rage. Collapsing onto the floor of that plywood cabinet, I felt I was flying to oblivion, that place where nothing hurts because I can't feel because this can't be happening because this can't be real because he is my father because I am his obedient daughter because fathers don't do this.

Fathers do this.

Fathers beat their daughters.

Fathers have murderous rage for their daughters.

Fathers loathe their daughters.

Fathers rape their daughters.

Or perhaps it was just this father, this daughter. Our destiny.

Didn't matter. Nothing mattered. I gave up. I submitted. I quit. With no escape, I fell into the bottomless hellhole depression of prey, stalked, trapped, wounded and bleeding out. Onward toward death with no escape. I fell into the trudging line of female ancestors bowing to our destiny.

Years later a therapist told me, "Yours is the most difficult abuse to recover from."

Hope did not exude from the therapist's words or her body. The finality of her pronouncement landed with a clunk in a familiar prison cell of hopelessness. Irreparably damaged goods. Broken glass. All the king's horses and all the king's men couldn't put Hollywog together again.

Troubled by the therapist's observation, I confided her words to Wendy, my Boston Public Schools social worker friend. Wendy smiled, donned her sassy attitude and wryly told me, "Holly, it seems to me your soul was pretty smart to get the hell out of there and to stay away from that crazy house. Your soul knew when it would be safe to come home. You are making it safe for your soul to come home."

Individual
Reflection Questions

---

1. Do children connect with the divine in different ways than adults?
    Can you recall and describe who God was to you as a child? How
    did your relationship with the divine evolve throughout your
    childhood and adulthood?

2. Institutions tell us who God is, teaching us to follow certain
    pathways to lead a holy life on earth. Have you experienced these
    pathways? If so, are they working for you? How much have you
    discovered your own pathways? How do you now see God, if you
    call the divine God?

3. From tragedy comes wisdom, if we are open to the lesson. What
    is a lesson you have learned from a tragedy, loss or other difficult
    time in your life? What do you think the author learned from
    this violent experience?

Book Group
Discussion Questions

1. When bad things happen to good people, how do you explain that to yourself? Who/what has helped you understand and perhaps accept this paradox? Why do good people get harmed?

2. At what age are we when we first get a true sense of our purpose? Some of us never feel we have fully found our purpose. What is your purpose, as much of it as you understand today?

3. What does discipline do for children? How were children disciplined in your family/experience? Is punishment effective with children? What messages do adults give children when we discipline or punish them?

PART 4
Betrayal

OUR NAMES MATTER

A young woman, whose surname is a hyphenated mongrel of cultures and sounds, often chooses to replace that whole megillah with a simple last name, usually selecting her partner's name. At the close of the wedding ceremony, priests, preachers or rabbis announce with flourish the empire just formed: *I give you Mr. and Mrs. Swinbourne, Mr. and Mrs. Hermilosa, Dr. and Mrs. Tran, Mr. Feldman and Dr. Feldman.*

I did not want to change my name. In fact, when I finally married at age thirty-one, I drafted a lawyerly contract with my psychologist husband-to-be clarifying to all that we would each keep our name. Our written contract, framed and placed prominently in our front entryway, enumerated agreements, how we would:

- acknowledge, work on and find help to resolve conflict;
- share costs of living;
- approach child-raising; and,
- each keep our given names.

I had already reclaimed my original family name and dropped the created name I was given at age three. I wasn't about to take another name.

First thing my new mother-in-law said to me when I next arrived at her home?

"Hello, Mrs. H---."

Traditions in tribes die hard.

Our names matter. Each part of our name holds our history, heritage, a memory, a legacy, an ancestor not to be forgotten, a namesake. Some of our names were stolen from us on slave galleons or hacked of ethnicity at Ellis Island.

My name is Holly Elissa Bruno. Simple, yes?

My name was chosen before I was conceived, the last of three children. With two daughters, my Sicilian patriarch father, Vincenzo Bruno, required a son. My mother wanted a son, "to spoil him rotten," boys being more valuable than girls. My parents determined I would be a boy named Greg. Greg Bruno.

Due to some mysterious-to-me warfare of blood types, for my parents to birth additional children after me would be dangerous. I was their youngest, their first son, their ultimate creation, and my name was Greg Bruno.

In my father's world, being born female stamped an unavertable fate: obedience, loyalty, caregiving, marriage, motherhood, cooking, sewing, cleaning, baking, tending to others' needs, anonymity, and never asking for much. My grandmother Addolorata Modello Bruno, raised in a convent in Caltanissetta, Sicily, aligned as well as she could with fate, and grew pregnant fourteen times (eight children survived).

Grandfather Michele proclaimed to the men in the *famiglia*, "I never let my wife go to bed with an empty stomach." He wasn't talking about a good meal.

Addolorata in her unsmiling wedding photo was tiny, raven haired, wasp-waisted. After twenty years of non-stop pregnancy, her long smooth hair kinked into untamable steel wool. Her surrendered waistline stretched her short body into a permanent A-frame. Her clothing was as matronly as Kate Smith's or Eleanor Roosevelt's shapeless dresses. Her angry, anxious dark eyes waited unceasingly for a person to listen to and understand her story.

Addolorata never spoke English. As a resident alien, she was in danger of being deported or sent to detention camps, as were other Italian and Japanese Americans. Most Italian immigrants were saved from that unholy round-up and banishment to camps because the

Italian-American owner of Chef Boyardee provided free pasta rations for the troops. And because the great Joe DiMaggio's parents would also have been sent away, Addolorata dodged that bullet.

But other bullets Addolorata did not dodge.

Addolorata in Italian means "our lady of sorrows." In Sicily, children were named after the saint on whose saint's day they are born. This is the only way I know my Nona's birthday was likely September fifteenth.

Sylvia, after Saint Sylvester, patron saint of New Year's Eve, could have been my name. Sylvia, I am told, was considered when my gender eliminated the favored name Greg Bruno.

My father never spoke of his mother, although he had been her firstborn. Aunt Pasqualina told us with reverence, "We always said, if you opened our mother's heart, you would find Vincenzo, 'Jim,' there." Vincenzo Bruno never pronounced Nona's name in our presence. When I asked her name, I was told she was "Peggy." At a family gathering recently, she was called "Dora."

I was never allowed to meet my Nona Addolorata. I would speak to her inside myself, wondering, *Can I have a whole afternoon with you, Nona? Can we bake something together in your kitchen?* I researched in the Encyclopedia Britannica, how she and I could surmount the disease that kept her "away." My father told me my grandmother "Peggy" had goiter. When I presented my case that goiter wasn't catching so could I please meet my Nona, my father's clanging response so slapped my brain, I knew never to ask again.

LEARNING TO LIE: WE ARE GERMAN

When in 1948, we were called together, we five Brunos in a circle, I was a fidgeting curiosity machine.

- What was going to happen?
- Did someone find Jacob's ladder?
- Were we moving to a lake where I could splash daily until the sun went to bed?
- Would clouds rain cats and dogs?
- Would money grow on trees?
- Perhaps our ship came in?

Somberly, my father, who shared little, spoke. I reminded myself to sit still, lock my knees together, smooth my smocked dress, and act like a young lady. My "felt sense" alerted me a big announcement was imminent. Goody gumdrops! A mystery would be revealed.

I couldn't understand everything he said; however, I got the point.

- We are German (Italian was never mentioned).
- Our name is Bruner, spelled B-r-u-n-e-r.
- My father's name is James William Bruner.
- He is married to Louise Riggs Bruner.
- My siblings and I, Holly Elissa Bruner, were not Brunos anymore.
- Our ancestors came from a land called Alsace-Lorainne, where people spoke German mostly. Sometimes they spoke another language, French.

Those people named Bruno we visited every holiday? We were not like them. We are the Bruners.

Dismissed we were. No questions allowed.

EVIDENCE TO THE CONTRARY IS INADMISSIBLE

Something was not right. The top of the Mason jar was not screwing on correctly. I felt a misfit in my body.

I climbed the stairs to find the cardboard "treasures" box in the back of the closet where special artifacts were thrown—photographs and bridge cards and newspaper clippings and even lockets of snipped hair. I dug to the bottom until I could feel the outline I sought. I clasped my hand onto the hard beads and pulled the bracelet up out of the treasures. I found it, my Corning Hospital baby bracelet, placed on my wrist at birth to identify me.

Each pink bead marked with one black letter spelled Holly Elissa B-r-u-n-o.

I carried my evidence carefully down the stairs. Respectfully as I could, I asked why was Bruno not my name?

My father's response was too swift, too harsh for my memory to handle. I can call up the feeling of that afternoon in the off-limits living room. I can feel the strangeness of the announcement. I can see my sisters nodding, nice young ladies they were. My mother was smiling almost triumphantly. But, as with many events and actions too slamming to recall, I cannot (yet) recall my father's spoken response. Perhaps he reacted with his fist.

> *Every time you lie,*
> *it brings me a little*
> *closer to goodbye.*
>
> **Anonymous**

BELLA SICILIA HOMELAND

From that day forward, until Spring 1977, I spelled my name B-r-u-n-e-r. That spring, I went to court with a former law school classmate representing me. Affirming that my change of name represented no fraud, I reclaimed B-r-u-n-o.

Shortly thereafter, I flew to Palermo, Sicily to discover Caltanisetta, my grandparents' hometown and sister city to Rochester, New York.

- *Caltanisetta*
- *Palermo*
- *Segesta*
- *Cefalu*
- *Erice*
- *Siracusa*
- *Agrigento*
- *Trapani*

The lyrically robust sounds and scents of the marketplaces welcomed me home.

I cried in bella Sicilia over steaming bowls of pasta sent to my table by families also dining at a neighborhood ristorante. Witnessing my wonder at their menu selections and seeming to understand, they shared their meals with me. Bambini beautifully clothed and exclaimed over were passed from adoring adult to adoring adult as toasts of vino were made.

I felt at home as I looked up at the mountains scaffolding the Temple of Segesta (420 BC), a temple untouched after it was erected. The conquering Greeks had left, abandoning their sacred temples to native Sicilians. The surface of the hill was gliding in movement. Undulating waves were pouring like honey down the mountainside to the mesmerizing music of bells. I asked myself, do I need water? Is the Sicilian sun baking my brain?

Then I saw shaggy goats coming down off the mountain in droves, each with a singing bell on her neck. In that timeless moment, I understood the poverty my grandparents had left behind and the riches they had abandoned to come to the New World.

Into America they brought their dreams and carried their sorrows. Both sorrows and dreams they would pass down to their progeny. The Brunos and the Modellos, mellifluous in enunciation, clanging in reality.

POSITIONS AVAILABLE: ITALIANS NEED NOT APPLY

My father, enraged at me for changing my name back to Bruno, refused to address me as Bruno until the 21st century after his wife had died. I wondered then if he sacrificed his heritage and native tongue not just to advance his career, but to quench my mother's need for status.

While my wasp cousins called me "wop," my mother's family complemented my sisters with approving words: you look like a Riggs. They excluded my dark self. If I asked, they would answer as if spitting out a fly: *You look like your father.*

In Boston, the Kennedys encountered signs in factory windows: "Positions available. Irish need not apply." In New York state, where four-fifths of Italian immigrants settled, employment notices hissed: "Positions available. Italians need not apply." When the 1930 census takers canvassed cities and villages to classify folk, they often checked Sicilians off as Negro. That autumn, Vincenzo Bruno trekked to Cornell University's engineering school as a needy scholarship boy, Negro on the census.

BLESSED IS THE DOOR

When I was born female on New Year's Eve, 1945, my father slammed in rage out of the hospital, perhaps to get drunk. My mother, in a bout of dissociation, psychosis or both, exacerbated by being drugged to deliver my overdue ten-pound nine-ounce self, could neither acknowledge nor care for me.

Nurses, perhaps noticing the uncelebrated baby, tied pink ribbons in my curls. My mother would later say, nurses tied the umbilical cord around my curls. I believed her. She was my mother.

No flowery pink birth announcement was mailed.

My name, Holly, was grabbed out of the air to mark my December birth. Elissa? No one remembered why Elissa was chosen for the girl child meant to be Greg.

I decided to use my whole name, Holly Elissa, because of its mellifluous "lee-uh-lee" sound and because I hoped Elissa in some way hearkened to my Sicilian roots. When my first book was published, Holly Elissa Bruno, MA, JD was the author.

My father never read my books. The little girl within me, Hollywog, ached for his praise. He would not read my books, even the ones that became bestsellers in my field. Nor the one that won the Silver Living Now award for books from any field that uplift the quality of life.

His dismissal choked my heart. When, as a child I told him he was choking my heart, he and my mother laughed.

'When a girl was born,' said the Hebrews, 'the walls wept.'

Japanese lullabies sang, 'If it's a girl, stamp on her.'

'Blessed is the door out of which goes a dead daughter,' was a popular Italian proverb.

The Evolution of Childrearing, Chapter 8. psychohistory.com

Today, I understand. With sadness and acceptance, I understand. I was not nor ever would be his Greg Bruner, the Sicilian patriarch's heir and intended prince.

"Blessed is the door out of which goes a dead daughter."

YOUR FAMILY ALWAYS LIED

"Your family has always lied to you and you need to accept that," a counselor in Arizona urged me. I was waiting, as we all were, for family week at the Meadows Recovery Center to begin. Family week meant our families would sit together in a safe place with counselors, sharing our truths without blaming or shaming. Each of us could say out loud what growing up in the family was like and how it affected us as adults. I yearned to hear and to share what had been so long unspeakable. I hoped love would pour out once the rocks of shame and pain were moved aside.

Family week at treatment centers is intended to bring together the recovering addict with her family to help prepare everyone to interact differently after release. I invited everyone: the Sicilians, the Scots, the Catholics, the Baptists. My dream of family healing through honesty and forgiveness was about to come true. Family members said they were coming.

Then the counselor told me, "No one in your family is coming."

I watched other families on the desert campus coming and going all week. I saw famous people and ordinary people. I saw families gathering to get help. I did not know how to grieve then. I did know I was angry, an emotion I had rarely allowed myself.

Each time you lie brings me closer to goodbye.

When I tell the story of my name now, people often respond: "What a horrible time that must have been for Italians, the newest immigrants. No wonder your father changed his name."

Of course, this observation is correct: Rejection, annihilation, demeaning always hurt the heart and harm the spirit. My father had faced discrimination, not been considered for jobs. My mother, who reminded us often she was "from good stock," was anxious for us all to be free of taint.

What no one talks about is the guillotine manner in which the re-naming took place. When Brunos became Bruners, we abandoned our identity, accepted a false ethnicity, gave up a rich heritage, and were commanded to unquestionably accept a lie as the truth. Consequences ensued.

Our family never would gather in the circle of truth-telling, lancing buried caches of shame and blame, bleeding free of our lies to welcome love.

Individual Reflection Questions

1. Reflecting on each of your names, from first to surname, middle name(s) if you have one(s), perhaps confirmation name, what is the history behind that name and the meaning of the name itself? What cultures and ethnicities and histories does your name represent? What matters most to you about your name and what do you like best about it?

2. Is your ethnicity or culture a dominant one or one that faced discrimination or both? What are stories your older relatives told about their experiences being raised within family traditions? Which traditions do you value and honor? What have you eliminated?

3. Did your family lie to you? What happened? How did you work that through inside yourself? Can families be honest with one another? What happens if they are not?

Book Group
Discussion Questions

1. Is your family historically a patriarchy where men have the power, or a matriarchy, where women make ultimate decisions, or both? Has that changed over the years? Are the cultures and practices of patriarchies different from matriarchies? If so, how?

2. What would cause a family member to be disowned or kicked out of your family? Has that ever happened? What is expected of you as a "good family member"?

3. If your family has secrets, or "dirty linen" that cannot be "aired outside the family," what is the reason behind keeping that private? Do you agree with your family's stance? Is keeping family secrets possible or desirable today especially given technological advances?

PART 5
Every Girl
for Herself

I devised ways to survive. In a family controlled by fear, we sisters barely bonded. Each of us worked laboriously to make it through the day and wake up to buckle down the next morning. The next morning, we knew the drill: Act as if nothing had happened in the night.

"You didn't see that, daughter."

The demand to bring accolades home to our parents required us to outdo one another.

Our family was pure patriarchy until my mother's insanity flared. Then her hellish out-of-body moaning or rage terrified us all into submission, cowing even my father. Did matriarchy prevail when my mother's insanity took control? No. When my mother flipped to a trapped wild animal, or a raging banshee, she was all hellfire, all damning, all terrifying. As with my father's rage, my mother's rage was the antithesis of a nurturing safe haven. My mother didn't wield power. Her insanity did.

Either way, rage-aholics ruled 12 Orchard Drive. We were fed a steady diet of fear. Girls possessed no worth beyond polishing the family image to outsiders. Variations from that theme were not tolerated. We obeyed two family mottos:

- *Grin and bear it.* Complaining, talking back, feeling sorry for ourselves, or not smiling were not tolerated. Reminders that "no one wants to see a frown on your face" sparked automaton smiles.

- *Brains, beauty and personality.* Bring home all A's, appear white-gloved, lady-like, and sunny. That was the spoken command. The unspoken command, "make us appear above suspicion especially to ourselves," produced three practiced image-managers.

My sisters earned A's and were "good girls." When I started South Corning Elementary school (Mrs. Bebout's domain) at age four, I bumped into little leeway to express myself. One sister had cornered the "perfect daughter" market, the other sister held tight to the "brilliant" and "prom queen pretty" market. With brains and beauty already claimed, I was left to deliver on the personality requirement. Outside the house, I had personality in spades. My problem was, I had no guidance on how to temper, hone or gain perspective on my personality. I was wild.

Hollywog proclaimed herself the sassy acrobatic tomboy, climbing trees, wrestling with boys, pretending confidence in her red cowgirl outfit, and playfully charging at Halloween parade-goers in my "Ferdinand the Bull" disguise. One time, playing the good Queen of Hearts in a play at the public library, I felt unsafe. Expressing vulnerability was scary for me. I did it, with difficulty.

Being a girlchild in 1950s conservative upstate New York meant squeezing into rigidly defined gender roles. But I wasn't having any of it! I refused to sacrifice the freedom of my outdoors self: in *my* forests, meadows and brooks, I claimed my curious, playful, laughing, hopeful, strong and free Hollywog self.

I pushed the limit of those confining gender boundaries until discipline at school triggered punishment at home. When my second-grade teacher Mrs. DeSilva was about to spank me for something another child had done, I hightailed it to the other side of the classroom. Mrs. DeSilva ran after me. Classmates cheered and whooped at the spectacle. When Mrs. DeSilva became winded, she announced I would stay after school for two weeks writing "I will not disobey" in white chalk over and over until I had filled the dusty chalkboards. For some untold reason, my mother didn't tell my father about that. If she had, out would have come the belt with the sharp metal buckle.

When my neighborhood friend Janie's oldest brother, Dick, tried to bully me, I took him on. Wrestling him feistily, my thin wrist snapped. I felt the bone crack and refused to cry. Dissociating from my body was by then a deeply honed skill. I announced with dignity or perhaps hauteur I was going to the doctor, turned and walked down the street to get a ride from my mother.

When my mother told me to forsake Mary Catherine Berhannon as my best friend, warning "Someone's going to get hurt," I silently refused. Mary Catherine and I kept each other laughing through boring classes by secretly passing outlandish notes back and forth. Our friendship made school fun. We were class cut-ups. Eventually, the school's tracking system split Mary Catherine and me up. Mary Catherine was not considered for gifted and college preparation classes. Mary Catherine was black and therefore had little chance her many gifts would be seen.

GOTCHA GOD

My heart has always created its own beat or marched to a different drummer. Rhumbas, sambas, twist, Macarena. My heart beat in its own universe. I was used to it.

I also got used to the routine of doctors and "Bible ladies" setting up shop in my elementary school classrooms in the 1950s. No notes were sent home to parents announcing these classroom take-overs. I don't recall that we children were given notice or choice. Of a sudden, a teacher would command us to line up for Dr. Purple or Dr. Ober, or sit attentively for Bible lady. Opting out was not imaginable.

Bible lady took over class more regularly than doctors, armed with her felt board of cut-out moveable biblical personalities and animals. In addition to black-bearded shepherds and blue-eyed

Jesus, Bible lady brought dark clouds and thunderbolts to convey her "gotcha-God" message.

"The wages of sin is death" (Romans 6:23). This Bible lady was no fun. She reminded me of my born-again sour-faced relatives in Olean who gave "being saved" a dreary name.

If we didn't understand her words, we were stun-gunned by her thunderclap message: sinners have no future. Sinners are likely to be struck down skipping home from school. God and Santa Claus shared that punitive pedagogy.

"You better watch out. You better not pout. You better not cry. I'm telling you why…"

I heard the same message at home.

"He knows what you are thinking. He knows when you're awake. He knows when you've been bad or good, so be good for goodness' sake!"

My mother would imply, "God's got eyes in the back of his head." There will be no escape.

Sinners were "trapped in the hands of an angry God." Ethan Frome was struck down, wasn't he? We later read about him in English class. The childless man with the witchy wife chose one blissful moonlight moment to toboggan with another woman who dared smile. Disaster struck the other woman. Her crashed, paralyzed, silent self would forever after drool in Ethan Frome's living room, tended by his still dreadful wife. There is no escape.

TELL YOUR PARENTS, MISSY

My turn was coming for the doctor's examination. When I was urged forward from the line to stand straight in front of the doctor, I stepped forward. Permission to stick out my tongue "ahhhhhhhhhh" for his popsicle stick was fun and prevented me from gagging. I pushed the boundary and crossed my eyes to win a laugh from my friends in line.

Watching the doctor's pensive face as he listened to my heart through his stethoscope was also appealing. Like most traumatized children, I had become expert at reading nuanced subtleties of body language:

- Was Mother slipping through the floorboards into depression or morphing into her moaning-demon self?

- Were Father's always red-gold embers of rage being fanned into a violent out-of-control flare-up?

- Was a sister scheming to "rat out" another sister to curry favor for herself?

- Was the doctor going to dismiss me as perfect or did his pinched face forewarn of trouble brewing?

The doctor listened again, like a robin cocking its head toward a worm. Without meeting my eyes, the doctor turned away dictating to his note-taking nurse: "Heart murmur, micro-murmur. Tell your parents, missy, to take you to the doctor."

That threw me into panic. We were not supposed to call attention to ourselves in any way. Having to bother my parents with the school doctor's assessment troubled me. I couldn't imagine how I could tell them. And worse, if something were wrong with me, they would be angry with me.

My mother's deep red scar on her inner hip had taught me to keep my mouth zipped. When I asked her how she got the scar, she responded that she had fallen down in the cinders and scraped her leg "wide open." When I asked why the scar was shaped like a scooped-out hole, she admitted her wound had likely become infected. Then I asked, "Why didn't the doctor help you?"

Looking down, she said flatly, "I didn't want to bother my mother."

THOU SHALT NOT GET SICK

Translation: *Don't get sick. If you do, keep it to yourself. Do not bother your parents. Child, heal thyself in silence.*

I soon discovered the fierce accuracy of this "don't bother your parents" directive. A lung-chilling upstate New York winter socked me with a commanding cough that wracked my chest. I could not run without coughing. I couldn't catch my breath. Sweaty and worn out, I did what was expected: Don't complain. Do your schoolwork during the week and your chores on Saturday.

This cough that owned me began to terrify me. My ebullient energy seeped like flour out of a motheaten sack. When December holidays finally came, I was dragging. Could barely stay awake during the drive to Rochester, New York, to first visit my Aunt Esther and her husband, Jerry. By now I was nauseous. When Aunt Esther's bathroom door was locked, I rushed out the back door to throw up in the snow. I must have passed out.

I was lifted out of the snow by an older cousin's husband who was out back for a smoke. This relative was a social worker for the state. He carried me into the house and insisted my parents get me medical care.

In the unfamiliar doctor's office, I came to during a strong disagreement.

This child belongs in a hospital. She has, at the very least, acute bronchitis. She is in danger.

We had relatives to visit. My parents couldn't be bothered by a sick child. They would not consent to my being hospitalized.

I was deposited from couch to couch at various relatives' houses or apartments. I slept all the time. Pills from the doctor were so huge, I could swallow them only if my mother embedded them in a teaspoon of spun honey. I don't recall much of those months recovering, except I was left alone in a bed with a bucket beside me on the floor and told to call out after I had thrown up. Once, too weak to get to the bucket, I threw up on the sheets. When I called my mother, I watched disgust and impatience contort her face.

Those who had been traumatized and subsequently developed PTSD did not modify their accounts: their memories were preserved intact essentially forty-five years after the war ended.

Bessel van der Kolk

To this day, my bodily reaction to injury or illness is fear, denial, despair and a dark mood.

Today, I call a doctor. Often reluctantly and fearfully, yet I call. Taking action helps. I connect with another person, share my fearsome burden, ask for help. I receive help.

Breaking all those childhood commandments not to request help, I straighten my shoulders, making room for my heart.

CATCH THAT ONE, SHE'S RUNNING!

I learned to fear doctors and dentists, with their absolute control over children's bodies. Without Novocain covering our pain, children of the 1950s endured metal drilling into the nerves of our teeth. As elementary school children, we were bused to the high school and lined up single-file down a long brick corridor. The polio epidemic was raging. My best friend, Claire G., was hospitalized with polio and very ill.

Gamma globulin injections were the order of the day. The syringes harbored what looked like poop to me, or nauseating bloody scabs liquidized into the largest needle my young eyes had ever seen. No! I could not bear being forced again to do something that terrified me. Run!

Public health technicians caught me, restrained me, forced me facedown onto a gurney, and yanked up my dress to stab a long thick needle full of seething gamma globulin into my right buttocks. Just as dismissively, the orderlies set me on my feet, pulled up my panties, pulled down my dress and pushed me ahead in the line. I froze for days, terrified I would die. I had no one I could tell, even if the words would form. I had no one to tell who would care who might help. My body kept that score too.

My Claire of the long blonde hair died of polio. I was not allowed at her funeral, although I sneaked down to the church to try to wave goodbye through the windows.

When Jonas Salk, creator of the polio vaccine, was asked who owned the patent to his vaccine, he replied, "There is no patent. Could you patent the sun?"

That polio epidemic terrified families nationwide with Black Plague force.

SURVIVAL OF THE TOUGHEST

When my oldest sister, Karen Jeannette, pinched me vise-like on the down-low with her long hard oval nails, I (not Karen) got hit for making noise. Karen feigned first-born righteous innocence. No one wanted to hear why I screamed. Silenzio! Silence! A child is at best seen, never heard. Karen brandished her weapons in triumph.

Injustice beleaguered me. I never could bear injustice. Why was I harmed twice? Pinched and struck. What was I to learn from being hit? The need for justice elbowed me.

To protect myself, I created and executed a plan: grow out my nails. Grow my nails long and hard like Karen's long hard nails. Then one fine day, clip them jagged and sharp as dragon's teeth.

When Karen circled 'round for her next hit, I planted myself, holding high my clawful weapons for Karen alone to notice. I used no words. Silenzio! One turgid ten-finger gesture nailed it.

Machiavelli applauded my triumph. Karen did not pinch me again. She turned to other methods.

As an adult Karen forgot every last moment of our childhood. If I had told her this dragon nail memory, she would have looked at me quizzically, innocently as a child in a home that was safe.

TRAUMA MADE BEARABLE BY DISSOCIATING

Dissociative amnesia is a type of dissociative disorder that involves inability to recall important personal information that would not typically be lost with ordinary forgetting. It is usually caused by trauma or stress.
⁓ *David Spiegel,*
Stanford University School of Medicine

My oldest sister became a mistress of dissociation, the process of leaving our bodies when trauma threatens. Karen's forgetting is called "dissociative amnesia."

Likewise, when I was beaten, I blacked out, an extreme form of dissociation wherein the body plays dead to protect itself. Before I blacked out, I imagined my soul flying away to a safe and sacred place where I could not be beaten and where I could be safe forever.

Let us forget,
with generosity,
those who
cannot love us.

Pablo Neruda

That was another way to dissociate.

Although Karen and I both were skilled at dissociation, we differed in one crucial way: she forgot. I remembered. I kept a journal that has informed this book. In childhood moments when violence was about to strike, I said to myself, 'Remember this. One day, this will help.'

My memories, like crumbs leading through a secret forest, have helped me find my way home. My sister, sadly, did not regain her memory. She lost more and more of it before she died. For Karen, I was sad for years.

LITTLE RED JOURNAL ENTRIES

My father has hurt me in a violent act. The pain is bad, the betrayal sharper. I find courage to tell him, "I am going to run away because hurting me isn't right."

"Don't leave; I couldn't live without you, daughter," he implores.

The rest of my life, I feel responsible for keeping him alive as his rigid body begins to fail him. In high school every time I hear a siren, my pounding heart convinces me my father is in the ambulance. I must get to him.

He uses this to meet his needs.

"Come massage my chest," he commands, "I think I'm having a heart attack."

Forcibly, my hands massaging his chest are shoved lower. I disappear in dissociation. To this day, the scent of tweedy woolen trousers disturbs me.

One of my high school classmates was shot dead by a fellow classmate in a lover's battle at their trysting hut on a nearby hill behind our house. Sirens wailing from then on doubly terrorized me. Because the lovers were male, no one in the community talked to children about the murder. In the days before trauma counseling for students, we muddled through. At the funeral, I choked with panic attacks. My wooded sanctuary lost its innocence, was no longer my safe-haven.

I HAVE THREE LOVELY DAUGHTERS

"Congratulations! That's quite an accomplishment by your daughter Holly."

I was so unused to being praised, I would hold still, riveted by positive words and the grace of a compliment. Could someone have seen my effort, noticed my success and congratulated me out loud? I yearned to hear positive words. I sunned myself in the glow of the moment before my father extinguished it.

I learned to heed my father's advice, "expect the worst." Bruner girls were allowed neither self-confidence nor pride. Joy was smashed by my father's predictably growled warning, "I have three lovely daughters."

My father's pronouncement terminated the compliment. He never said thank you. His words and commanding demeanor were a don't-push-me-any-further warning. He permitted no praise for me as an individual. Not only might the praise go to my head, praise was not permissible. I had no identity beyond being my father's daughter, one of three. He deserved the praise, not us.

We are people who need to love, because love is the soul's life, Love is simply creation's greatest joy.

Hafiz

I left those moments feeling discarded, seen one moment, unseen the next. I expect people learned not to give us compliments. I learned not to hope for any.

COMMAND PERFORMANCES

Every Sunday before church, we three daughters endure my father's inspection as we walk ladylike down the stairs into the small foyer, to be told whether he approves. If he does not approve of how we present ourselves, we are sent back up the stairs to get it right.

My sisters enjoy this. They are approved and like his attention. I am angry to be rejected. I come to hate the procession before the judge. I am dark; I am "stick body" thin; I am ethnic. My father calls me his "exotic one." I sense that being exotic is neither safe nor respectable.

ULTIMATE AUTHORITY

Times come when truth enters the room. When truth flows, I have learned not to stop the flow even when fear fights to prevail. My body, which has kept the score, was used to shutting truth down.

As long as I do not remember the truth, I can live in the pretend zone of my sister Karen. Her father was a saint. Or, in the reality of my other sister for whom our father was her "rock." She clutched her fist to her heart as she said that. "He was my rock" is a direct Christian allusion. Peter was the rock upon which the church was built.

For my sisters, our often-insane mother was demon. Our father was savior.

I understand that need. Mother's haunting out-of-body episodes were unbearable and inescapable. Someone had to be savior of the little terrorized children.

My father, my abuser, was not my savior. To this day, I do not know if he sexually abused my sisters as he sexually used me. However,

I know and recall all too well the sound of my father's fists hitting one sister, and the resounding thump as he threw her against the wall. I remember my mother's scream. "You'll kill her, Jim!"

I remember my sister falling into bed in our shared room. I remember our silence. We could neither cry nor talk, for fear he would enter our room and resume. Sorrow spoke instead, shrouding the room with inexpressible grief.

MY FATHER WAS MANY THINGS

My father was many things. He stored his celestial charts beneath the cupboard in the kitchen, pulling out those scrolls to determine which boy scout could win his astronomy badge. My father held old instruments with pale green-yellow fluid to measure a line's straightness. He built our house literally from the ground up. He ran for and eventually was elected mayor of our village.

My father smiled at me once. I was perhaps three, left to cavort freely at the unprotected edge of the excavated rectangular earthen pit of our basement. I watched my father's competence and marveled at his work, transforming earth to edifice, commanding wildness into order. He looked up for a moment at my awestruck child's face. And he smiled. My father smiled at me. I can feel his smile now. I do not recall him smiling at my innocence again.

As I live in that timeless moment now, I am grateful for it, as a child is grateful for lights on a Christmas tree or snow slanting under a street lamp.

I also no longer hold onto that moment as pure. I know the complexity of my father's messages to me. Few if any of those messages were about love. I am quite sure my father did not know how to love me. He passed on the woundedness he knew. This was his legacy to me. This is the legacy I seek to change as I write this book.

My extended family converged on the coast of Maine for my October, 1977, wedding. Everyone was celebratory, perhaps relieved the errant daughter at age 31 was at last settling down. Sitting across from my parents at an upscale restaurant on Falmouth's rocky shore, I heard them repeat one of their mantras, "We're so grateful we never had to discipline you girls. You were all so well-behaved."

Without censuring myself I blurted, "But you beat us."

Equally uncensured, my father did what he had never done before and never would do again.

"Can you forgive me, daughter," he asked, placing his hand on top of mine.

I responded as honestly as I was able.

"I guess I have to," I acknowledged.

As was our way, we closed down in a flash, scurrying from awkward intimacy. Later, my mother called me, scolding.

"Your father will not speak to you again. You used words to hurt."

As was my way, I blamed myself ever after. I should have forgiven him. What is wrong with me? I did not ask, "Why did I respond as I did," because I knew the answer.

As was my way, I told the truth. I knew I was expected to forgive him; however, in that raw moment, I was not ready. My broken heart could not suddenly sew itself together in time to release the pain my father's abuse, incest and disdain had caused me.

That healing would require another forty years.

PERFECTION IN TRIPLICATE

I conjured up many ways to help my mother smile. That was my job, serving as her cheerleader, her clown, her fop, her playmate, her coworker, her sidekick, her shopping mate. I could not let her begin to slide down into her dark place. The sounds of bedlam she bellowed suffocated me.

Mother (we were not allowed to call her Mommy) shopped and I followed, skipping along when I could. Often, we devoted entire days to her shopping. Iszard's and Rosenbaum's, the "big" department stores in Elmira, focused my mother. She had purpose. She was on a hunt.

She had shopping rules:

- Never buy the first thing you see that you like.
- Go to other stores to find it cheaper.
- Check every option before at last returning to get what you wanted from the beginning.
- Buy only one special item.
- Save your money.

Shopping was as close to a science as anything my mother did besides cleaning. Cleaning was a science too. Orderly rituals prevailed.

My mother taught me, for example, never to leave the house without circling round the house at least twice to test every door and every window to make sure it was locked. Checking each lock three times around was better: perfection in triplicate.

CHORE DAY, SORE DAY

Saturday was chore day. We each had our jobs. Each job had to be perfectly executed. If I was slow or unskilled, my mother would snatch what I was working on out of my hands and scold, "If you want something done right, do it yourself."

She also yelled at us in German, or was it Yiddish? One of her frequent reproaches as she inspected our work was the equivalent of, "What do I have? Pigs for daughters." We could not leave the house Saturday until our chores met mother's impossible standard.

She screamed all day. Screamed. All. Day.

Even my father was cowed. He, in his work khakis, met my eye once across the kitchen while mother pontificated in screams. Father stood silent in one doorway as I paralleled him in the opposite doorway. We looked at one another with understanding.

We did not roll our eyes. She would have seen that. The acknowledgement of mutual resentment helped me. We were peers, my father and I, survivors of something dark I, at least, did not understand.

His eyes flashed, "She's crazy, so pretend to pay attention to everything she says as if it were gospel." I joined him in pretending.

The youngest in the house, my ears couldn't withstand the scorch of red-hot lava poured into them by each scream. I determined to take on the onerous task of scrubbing both bathrooms. Why? Bathrooms were for privacy. I could shut the doors while scrubbing to blunt the intensity of her screaming. Silver faucets sparkled. Mirrors had the clarity of open windows. Toilet bowls dazzled. I polished surfaces until no flaws could be detected. Only when I sneaked out of the first-floor bathroom to silently bound up the stairs to the second bathroom, might I get caught and become pincushion to her screams.

Today, if a woman raises her voice in anger or in pain, my ears burn hot, as if a cone of red coals were poured into them. For most of my life, I have avoided women raging. I almost never scream. Many times I have dreamed I could scream.

ROSENBAUM'S, OF COURSE

Shopping in nearby Elmira was wearying for my three- and four-year-old legs. But, shopping meant no screaming. My mother, intent on her hunt, would not scream at me in public. Shopping was a reprieve.

Department stores in the 1940s captured another world.

White-gloved elevator attendants pulled metal accordion doors to the side to admit and release us on different floors. I loved the swoosh of plastic vacuum tubes that catapulted folded paper back and forth. Was money being catapulted through those tubes? Receipts? I didn't totally understand, but the sound and movement fascinated me. I watched those clear plastic tubes as if they might whisper the secrets of the gods of commerce.

Sometimes my mother would notice I was with her. When she did, she and I would break for lunch at the store restaurant. Tuna fish on white bread without crusts with sweet pickles. Sunny egg salad with pimento. Or simply a "Mexican" sundae: Spanish peanuts, hot fudge, vanilla ice cream. Food became a reward.

One time mother walked off forgetting my sister and I were with her. We waited for her return. There was something familiar about being alone. My sister grew anxious and adults noticed. When mother was found, she didn't seem to notice us. But the store's crisis was settled. Reuniting lost children with parents was their job. Just as the law seeks to reunite families, the store had done its part and had no further responsibility for abandoned children. Courts do the same: send hurting children back to the families that inflict the hurt. Children get the message.

WHO WAS MY MOTHER?

My mother's accomplishments were a clean house, perfectly folded laundry, rigorous church attendance, devotion and donations to evangelist Billy Graham, looking put-together and beautiful, shopping for bargains and producing ladylike daughters.

Sometimes, at her monthly bridge club, she and her partner would win, another accomplishment. I never learned bridge. Children were not allowed in the living room on bridge club night, card tables set with bridge mix chocolates, pastel mint pastilles, coffee cups with cherry red lipstick, cigarette smoke, and Ginny Sullivan's horsey laugh followed by her phlegmy smoker's cough.

My mother once performed interpretive dance while working in Olean, New York, her home town, at Cabot Gas company where she added numbers, having left school in tenth grade. Like Isadora Duncan, my mother in the early 1930s garbed herself in flowing materials, not quite diaphanous, but sheer nonetheless. In one remaining photograph, she sits in the middle of a big band-like orchestra, Ginger Rogers without Fred Astaire.

The sepia photo is at once lovely, nostalgic and alarming. My mother's head is cut out of the photograph, as if a guillotine had haunted the stage. I did not understand where my mother's head went and I was likely frightened, but I couldn't show fear when I asked my mother, "Why did you cut your face out of the photograph?"

She responded, "I didn't like my looks."

To this day, I can see my mother's dance performance photo with the head-sized hole in the middle without closing my eyes.

Individual
Reflection Questions

1. What were visits to the doctor or dentist like for you as a child? What helped you feel safe and soothed there, or what might have helped you? Has patient care, especially of women and children, evolved to where you would like it to be?

2. When mental health is an issue in a family, how can the family deal with that equitably and lovingly? How can mental illness effectively be explained to children? What helps family members accept and support mentally-challenged members while at the same time take care of themselves?

3. Did you feel your own parents or caregivers gave you mixed messages at times, perhaps saying one thing in words but acting the opposite of what they were saying? How did you make sense of that? What practices do you use when communicating your expectations to children?

Book Group
Discussion Questions

1. What public health scares have you faced in your lifetime? Did anything or anyone help you feel safe, protected and able to pull through the crisis? What, if anything, held you back from receiving the help you needed? Have you experienced trauma counseling after a public health crisis?

2. What can families do to help siblings accept and appreciate one another's differences? When conflicts and rivalries surface, what practices can families use to work through and resolve those differences? If you have participated in a "family meeting," or "intervention" what makes such gatherings successful?

3. When people, because of their own histories of woundedness, are unable to feel or show love, can you have a meaningful relationship with them? Hurt people hurt people; is passing on family dysfunction inevitable, or can the cycle be broken? If so, how?

PART 6
Up to the Balcony

*Our sorrows and wounds are healed only
when we touch them with compassion.*

~∞~

Buddha

Writing this book, I often need to stop, rest, tend my gardens, walk through the meadow, gather with friends, focus on my other work, read or creatively cook.

You too may need a break from my stories. Perhaps we both could take a rest from the narrative to climb to the balcony of perspective.

Survivors can change things; victims are forever at the mercy of others.

Notice how a traumatized person describes herself. Does s/he call herself a victim of an atrocity or a survivor of the atrocity? That one word tells you how the person sees herself and wants to be treated.

I am a survivor, not a victim. Victims are so beaten down, they abandon hope. I have felt the desperate hopelessness of the victim. Survivors are so beaten down, we choose hope. I was born with hope. No matter how impossible things got, I held on to the dream my life could get better. My colleague Luis shrugs, "Without hope, what have we got?"

Over the hilltops I believed a better life awaited me. And it did. Once I left that house and its poisonous ways behind, I experienced freedom in marvelous manifestations. I found my voice, my talents, my originality and my passion. Yet, sorrow buried deep demanded expression. I devoted my middle years to living the best life I knew how, succeeding in many ways. But sadness inside stalked me. In the end, I knew I could no longer run from truth. When Robert Frost wrote, "the best way out is always through" he penned the guiding principle for restoring my soul.

I accepted that I needed to ask for and accept help. I realized I could not heal on my own. I understood that the fierce traits I had developed to survive would not serve me if I wanted to live. I agreed with Thoreau, I did not want to come to the end of my life only to discover I had not lived.

At this pivotal point in the telling of my story, I want to share with you four resources that helped me regain the perspective I craved:

- Dr. Judith Herman's book *Trauma and Recovery* (1992) opened my heart and my vision to the deeper roots of trauma, both personal abuse and systemic abuse. I no longer felt I was the only one, the crazy one.

- Dr. Bessel van der Kolk's *The Body Keeps the Score: Brain, Mind and Body in the Healing of Trauma* (2014) affirmed my understanding of PTSD's complexity and of the professional as well as self-help that is available.

- The ACEs, Adverse Childhood Experiences Study (2008) confirmed my knowing that we survivors are legion and can free one another by speaking out.

- Tony A's *Laundry List* (1978) and The ACA (Adult children of alcoholic/dysfunctional families) big book (2006) provides me everyday strategies, steps and supports for the long recovery road I have chosen.

Toward the end of this book, I will share everyday practices that are transforming my life.

PLACING MY PERSONAL HISTORY IN CONTEXT

I had trouble breathing as I began reading Judith Herman's book in the early 1990s. Dr. Herman worked just down the street at Cambridge Hospital, a few blocks from my condominium. I had discovered a support group for anxiety sufferers at Cambridge Hospital facilitated by a gentle colleague of hers. Working with him and listening to fellow troubled professionals, I began to uncover the raw dread I had long buried. I shook much of the time, but I did not run from the group. It was a beginning.

When I read Herman's own amazement as she worked with survivors like me, I had to again remind myself to breathe.

After forty years of doing this work, I still regularly hear myself saying "That's unbelievable," when patients tell me about their child-hoods. They often are as incredulous as I am—how could parents inflict such torture and terror on their own child? Part of them continues to insist that they must have made the experience up or that they are exaggerating. All of them are ashamed about what happened to them and they blame themselves—on some level they firmly believe that these terrible things were done to them because they were terrible people (Trauma and Recovery).

I blamed myself, just as I had when my father took off with the hatchet to kill Timothy the cat. When children have no other role models, those children, Dr. Herman confirms, writhe in shame. My parents told me frequently, "You ought to be ashamed of yourself." I was ashamed of myself for being alive. How could I forget I had failed from birth to be the promised son both my parents needed to fulfill themselves?

SHAME ON ME

When I discovered Bessel van der Kolk's work, I felt relieved, for some reason, that he too was nearby in Boston working with clients like me. I couldn't stop reading.

As long as you keep secrets and suppress insights, you are fun-damentally at war with yourself. Hiding your core feelings takes an enormous amount of energy, it saps your motivation to pursue worthwhile goals, and it leaves you feeling bored and shutdown. Meanwhile, stress hormones keep flooding your body, leading to headaches, muscle aches, problems with your bowels and sexual functions, and irrational behaviors that may embarrass you and hurt the people around you. Only after you identify the source of those responses, can you start using your feelings as signals of problems that require your urgent attention (The Body Keeps the Score).

I had tried so many approaches to get better: prayer and meditation, yoga, working out, reading self-help books, taking rigorous courses, in-patient treatment for the disease of codependency, holding conversations with wise people. These too were only beginnings. Reading van der Kolk, like reading Herman, I began to understand that PTSD kills just as surely as a drug overdose, a stroke or a heart attack. I understood also that I had to say goodbye to self-destructive habits and learn new ways to live–not just survive.

van Der Kolk cited rampant domestic/familial abuse statistics in support of his theory "the real war is at home":

- One out of every five Americans is sexually molested as a child.
- One out of four is beaten by a parent to the extent that marks show on the body.
- One in three couples engage in physical violence.
- One quarter of Americans grew up with alcoholic relatives.

"The greatest source of our suffering is lies we tell ourselves," van Der Kolk concludes.

Lying to myself was only a short-term fix to a long-term problem.

When I studied the ACEs findings, I was overwhelmed. All of the illnesses that had plagued my family, the shortening of our lifespans, stabbed directly at my heart. More upsetting yet was the volume of children and families included in the study. We survivors were no longer an aberration, we represented a significant part of the American population. Most disturbing of all was to assess myself by the ACEs indicators below. My high score and low life expectancy did not surprise me, they saddened me. Only two answers I left unchecked:

#6. My parents had not divorced. Divorce, a sin, was not an option. My mother would not have survived a divorce.

#12. No one had gone to prison. My family needed to appear perfect, above reproach. No one would think of breaking the law, unless battering your children was against the law. My family thought that was a father's right. I did have drug dealer relatives; but, being white decreased their likelihood of detection or jail time.

If you wish to, work your way through this ACEs questionnaire.

What's your ACE (Adverse Childhood Experiences) score?
(Go to cdc.gov for scoring information.)
Prior to your eighteenth birthday:

1. Did a parent or other adult in the household often or very often... Swear at you, insult you, put you down, or humiliate you? Or, ACT in any way that made you afraid you might be physically hurt? No____. If yes, enter 1____.

2. Did a parent or other adult in the household often or very often...Push, grab, slap, or throw something at you, or ever hit you so hard that you had marks or were injured?
No_____. If yes, enter 1_____.

3. Did an adult or person at least 5 years older than you ever... Touch or fondle you or have you touch their body in a sexual way? Or Attempt to actually have oral, anal or vaginal intercourse with you?
No_____. If yes, enter 1_____.

4. Did you often or very often feel that...No one in your family loved you or thought you were important or special? Or Your family didn't look out for each other, feel close to each other or support each other?
No_____. If yes, enter 1_____.

5. Did you often or very often feel that...You didn't have enough to eat, had to wear dirty clothes, and had no one to protect you? Or Your parents were too drunk or high to take care of you or take you to the doctor if you needed it?
No_____. If yes, enter 1_____.

6. Were your parents ever separated or divorced?
No_____. If yes, enter 1_____.

7. Was your mother or step mother: Often or very often pushed, grabbed, slapped, or had something thrown at her? Sometimes, often, or very often kicked, bitten, hit with a fist or something hard? Or Ever repeatedly hit over at least

a few minutes or threatened with a gun or a knife?
No____. If yes, enter 1____.

8. Did you live with anyone who was a problem drinker or
    alcoholic, or who used street drugs?
    No____. If yes, enter 1____.

9. Was a household member depressed or mentally ill, or did a
    household member attempt suicide?
    No____. If yes, enter 1____.

10. Did a household member go to prison?
    No____. If yes, enter 1____.

The Centers for Disease Control's ACEs study uncovered a stunning link between childhood trauma and chronic diseases people develop as adults, as well as social and emotional problems. Heart disease, lung cancer, diabetes and many autoimmune diseases, as well as depression, violence, being a victim of violence, and suicide are likely our fate.

I never imagined I would live to be 73.

I couldn't picture my life after 21.

I wasn't sure I would make it to 17.

ANOTHER ASSESSMENT HITS HOME
*Fear is the cheapest room in the house. I would like
to see you living in better conditions.* ⌒ **Hafiz**

Cambridge, Massachusetts, was an enlightening place to live. I thrived there in so many ways. In Cambridge, I was introduced to and befriended members of the "recovery community," people who supported one another's healing from substance addictions like drugs, alcohol, and sugar, and helped one another face process addictions such as being a work addict, achievement addict, or codependent.

Codependents lack self-esteem and are addicted to the approval of others. I soon discovered I was a full-blown workaholic, achievement addict and codependent. Over time, I would learn the direct relationship between my traumatic upbringing and my process addictions. Along the way, I discovered a checklist of traits shared by survivors of dysfunctional and/or alcoholic families. Another punch to my heart! I read these *Laundry List* traits drafted in 1978 by survivor Tony A. (to maintain anonymity, people in recovery list only the first initial of their last name). On this assessment, my score is perfect.

Children of trauma world-over get through dark nights and anxious days by shielding ourselves with protective traits. You may have learned some of these yourself. Tony A., New York City stockbroker, son of a troubled mother and raging father, articulated the survival traits of children of trauma:

1. We became isolated and afraid of people and authority figures.

2. We became approval seekers and lost our identity in the process.

3. We are frightened by angry people and any personal criticism.

4. We either become alcoholics, marry them or both, or find another compulsive personality such as a workaholic to fulfill our sick abandonment needs.

5. We live life from the standpoint of victims and we are attracted by weakness in our love and friendship relationships.

6. We have an overdeveloped sense of responsibility and it is easier for us to be concerned with others rather than ourselves; this enables us not to look too closely at our own faults, etc.

7. We get guilt feelings when we stand up for ourselves instead of giving in to others.

8. We became addicted to excitement (fear).

9. We confuse love with pity and tend to "love" people we can "pity" and "rescue."

10. We have "stuffed" our feelings from our traumatic childhoods and have lost the ability to feel or express our feelings because it hurts so much (denial).

11. We judge ourselves harshly and have a very low sense of self-esteem.

12. We are dependent personalities who are terrified of abandonment and will do anything to hold onto a relationship in order not to experience painful abandonment feelings, which we received from living with sick people who were never there emotionally for us.

13. Alcoholism is a family disease; we became para-alcoholics (codependents) and took on the characteristics of that disease even though we did not pick up the drink.

14. (Codependents) Para-alcoholics are reactors rather than actors.

⌒ Tony A, The Laundry List, 1978

Of course, I feared authority figures. Adults were unsafe, unpredictable, lying, violent and out-of-control. I did not trust them. From infancy, I relied on myself to get through, to figure out how to stay alive.

Without models of maturity, we each fell into the only rut open to us: self-doubt, fear and self-hatred or grandiosity, imagining we were powerful in magical ways. Our path of perfectionism or underperforming spread out ahead of us, neither path leading us home. We did not have a home.

A child who feels unloved blames herself for being unlovable. When parents are enraged, the child believes she sparked their rage. When a child is beaten, she feels she deserves the blows. When a child is abandoned (again), she cannot bear the sorrow clawing at her weakened heart. She works to perfect her best self, the golden girl that wards off punishment by pleasing everyone in power. To survive, she learns to escape, self-medicate, self-annihilate or even sacrifice her soul.

As I left the confines of Corning, New York, and traveled over the hill tops at last, I discovered the life I had always wanted. Sadly, that fresh and precious life was to be marred by the survival traits I had learned, the panic disorder and complex PTSD I didn't know I had, and by my repetition of the some of the very behaviors I sought most to leave behind at 12 Orchard Drive.

Have you heard this expression? *Three-hundred and sixty degrees away from sick is still sick?*

Individual
Reflection Questions

1. Do the statistics presented by Dr. van der Kolk surprise you? Do you have people in your life that bear out these statistics? What would it take to lower these percentages and have less trauma in our culture(s)?

2. When you read the list of Adverse Childhood Experiences study questions, how did you feel? (I recommend you seek out the video of California Surgeon General Nadine Burke Harris's Ted Talk on ACEs, cited in the Bibliography, p. 260. If you listen, what did you hear in her Ted Talk that most affected you?

3. Were you surprised that addictions aren't just to substances such as drugs, alcohol and sugar, but that we can also be addicted to processes, including work addiction, perfectionism, driving ourselves to achieve or compulsively going online? Another definition of an addiction is "something we feel we have to lie about." What, if any, are your addictions?

Book Group
Discussion Questions

1. What do you think will happen next in Holly Elissa's life, given her early experiences and her hope? What might be the long-term effect of being raised the way she was? Are you still living out some of the ways you were taught as a child even though you would prefer to act differently?

2. "It is enormously difficult to organize one's traumatic experiences into a coherent account—a narrative with a beginning, middle and end" (van der Kolk). How does the way this book is organized (or not organized) affect you? Is hearing memories of a trauma survivor difficult? How possible is it for you to share memories of difficult times or trauma you have faced?

3. Survivors blame themselves. Why is that? How could a child believe she could be responsible for the actions of an adult? Survivors also have trouble trusting their own memories. What would help a survivor believe herself, stop blaming herself, or recall the truth she had buried?

PART 7

Adult in Body, Child Within

The Spring and the Fall
In the spring of the year, in the spring of the year
I walked the road beside my dear.
The trees were black where the bark was wet.
I see them yet, in the spring of the year.
He broke me a bough of the blossoming peach
That was out of the way and hard to reach.
In the fall of the year, in the fall of the year,
I walked the road beside my dear.
The rooks went up with a raucous trill.
I hear them still in the fall of the year.
He laughed at all I dared to praise,
and broke my heart in little ways.
Year be springing or year be falling,
The bark will drip and the birds be calling.
There's much that's fine to see and hear
In the spring of a year, in the fall of a year.
'Tis not love's going hurts my days,
But that it went in little ways.

Edna St. Vincent Millay

IT WENT IN LITTLE WAYS

I journeyed east at last over the hilltops from my hometown. Thrilled to begin my life.

Waving bittersweet goodbyes to best friends. Passionate to learn each day and sleep safely at night. I had cut my way out of the family's sticky web. Unlike nearby Cornell where my sisters studied, my college was distant enough that no one could "drop in" frequently.

In my new life, I took risks, faced up to failures, learned exponentially, laughed often, formed friendships that will last 'til our final breaths, found success. No longer stalked by namable demons, I strode down college pathways, greeting everyone by name.

Unnamable demons packed themselves in the crevices of my suitcase, and in unseen crannies of my brain. In 1963, Daniel Goleman had not identified the "amygdala hijack"–the experience of being taken over by fear. I did not know what an amygdala was; however, I felt its potency. When stress inflamed those primitive, autonomic, "fight, flight, freeze, fawn" knee-jerk defense glands, my confidence deflated, my joy was smashed on the cement like finely blown and etched Steuben crystal.

I fought the devastation. I refused to quit on my dream. I had not heard about the "geographical cure" for trauma, the belief that we will be free of PTSD if we change locations or relationships, work or life focus. Even more haunting, I did not have a term or diagnosis for what ailed me.

I did have hope for a happier life in a more receptive world. On that, I would not quit.

IN THE FALL OF THE YEAR

Seventeen I was in 1963, off to college in New Brunswick, New Jersey, Douglass College of Rutgers University. No one I knew had heard of it.

Douglass was perfect for me. Bright, accomplished, self-defining and inspiring women led the college and were our professors. Male professors were dedicated to women's intellectual, leadership and character development.

Rigorous Douglass's liberal arts curriculum paralleled the "Seven Sisters" colleges (female equivalent of the Ivy League), while being unencumbered by class privilege and significantly higher tuition. We were required to demonstrate competence in every area needed for well-informed leadership (sciences, math, political science, philosophy, art, music, foreign language, public speaking, modern dance, swimming, health), while meeting exhaustive requirements for our chosen major. Hard yet enchanting work for this seventeen-year-old whose family had never asked her opinion and whose teachers had expected her to memorize facts.

Everything about Douglass demanded that I:

- Think clearly, originally and creatively
- Advocate for constructive change and social justice
- Be well informed, bold, direct, articulate and persuasive
- Take a hard look at myself to discover what contribution I could make

The opposite of what I had been raised to be, this is what my women's college experience required. I dived in. Floundered some academically, thrived socially. Dived deeper.

I discovered a new family of intense, collegial and humorous women with backbone, dedicated to learning, maturing, excelling and making a difference. Most of us were children or grandchildren of immigrants, first generation in our families to go to college. Failing was not an option.

TO EXCEL, I FAILED

On academic probation for failing calculus second semester of my first year, I transformed into a scholar, making the Dean's List sophomore year. I could not bring shame to my family.

When I graduated in 1967 and headed off to graduate school, my closest friends and I joked we would meet again in the feminist old folks' home and kick up another storm. Oh, the conversations we would have!

We had memorized "Gaudeamus Igitur" in Latin to sing along at our graduation. Who does that?

When I froze during my calculus final my first year, unable to read the page, "blue book" empty of required calculations, I asked for help. Douglass had a psychiatrist on staff in the infirmary. My brilliant friend, Linda, found him helpful. I told

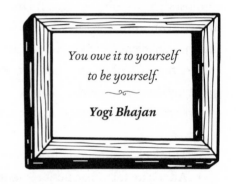

You owe it to yourself to be yourself.

Yogi Bhajan

him how the pages of the calculus exam melted in my vision, how I could not read the questions or breathe. We had no language then for panic attacks or complex PTSD flashbacks. I assumed I was crazy like my mother. Speaking up about my inner roiling was forbidden. So, I asked for help in the most adult and professional way I knew.

The psychiatrist summarily dismissed me: *I have students who are in danger. You are highly functional. I cannot fit you in.* I walked out of Jameson Infirmary relieved at first to hear I was highly functioning, yet sorrowful at heart. I was crazy like my mother, functionally crazy, my brain flatlining under stress.

My father was right: I was stupid. And, he would add, useless, third rate, broken from birth.

I shall become my psychotic mother. I cannot stop that inheritance.
My mother, my grandmothers and who else before them? Crazy as
loons, these women. Crazy in the night, the dark nights of the soul.

NO CONGRATULATIONS, NO APOLOGY

I recalled a year prior, hearing my father's pronouncement the
morning of the New York State Regents Scholarship examination,
a comprehensive competitive full-day test that determined who
statewide would be awarded university scholarships. My father
unequivocally declared I would fail.

His shaming disdain sucker punched me. On the bus to school, a
sizzle of outrage flickered inside me. In that moment, I determined
I would knock the top off the Regents exam. I steeled myself to focus
my outrage productively.

When scholarship winners were announced over Corning Free
Academy's public address system, my name came first. I shook,
holding myself back from leaping up or choking up.

I did not tell my father I had excelled, not failed, as he had ordained.
When the list of scholarship winners appeared in the *Corning Leader*,
my father said flatly from behind his newspaper, "Oh, I see you got
a scholarship."

"Yes," I said.

He offered no congratulations, no apology. I did not expect either.

SELF-UNFULFILLING PROPHECY

I had catapulted to the other side of the hills, relieved, grateful, on
a quest for a meaningful life. I reveled in my freedom and marveled
at my choices. I made friends, was elected to leadership positions
like class president. To pay expenses, I hefted trays circled with eight
weighty dinner plates in the dining hall for our sit-down dinners.

Speaking French, I served the French table. I chose "Development of Soviet Ideology," comparative religion, and other courses my family would not allow had they known.

Liberal arts was created for me.

I fell in love with learning. As Rilke had exhorted, I had learned "to love the questions."

I rose early on Saturdays, joked with friends in the dining hall, then we walked to the "libe" to ensconce ourselves in our haven of books, to puzzle through conundrums, tackle research projects, create paper after paper, and prepare to speak up in our demanding classes.

We played too and, on occasion, allowed ourselves a Saturday evening at the local pub, or on a date at nearby Rutgers or Princeton. Just as a frothy wedding cake dress was not my goal, finding a partner was not my quest. My task was to find my niche, uncover what I loved, and determine how I could use my education to make the difference I felt called to make.

In graduate school at the University of North Carolina-Chapel Hill, I thrived for a while, finding graduate literature courses breezy after the intensity of my undergraduate studies. I pioneered the way when professors and students at the traditionally male university (the undergraduate school only began to admit women the year I arrived on campus) showed bias against women.

When, for example, I confronted one professor about his statement that we women in the class were seeking our Mrs., not our PhD., I confronted him alone. The other women, mostly from southern women's colleges, agreed with him. One perfectly made-up and coifed woman said in her sweet Southern accent, "He's right, I want to become a teacher so I can devote myself to my children and return to teaching when they are older."

There it was: these women accepted what my sisters and I had been counseled to do: earn a teaching degree, so if something happens to your husband you can support your family.

Unlike Douglass, where professors believed in us, Chapel Hill English department professors took little interest I could see in women's advancement. Walking across the campus quadrangle with my first true love, Hank, a Yale alumnus also working on his doctorate, a professor joined "us." He talked only with Hank, discussing placements for Hank when he graduated. The old boy network would set Hank up for a plum position. Again, I spoke up, letting the professor know I, too, was ready to get in line to pluck one of those plums. The professor quickly walked away.

That was the way of the 1960s: women had our place. The lone woman completing her doctorate was advised to focus on children's literature. Soon enough the walls of the graduate library began to crowd in on me. Our study carrels were in windowless below-ground catacombs, unlike those at Douglass, where pine trees waved from the windows outside and light flooded abundantly through ample skylights. Panic attacks, and PTSD flashbacks to childhood tortures and abandonment, sabotaged my concentration. When the Graduate Education School, where I had a teaching fellowship, offered me placement at West Charlotte Senior High School, an all-black institution, I decided to complete my master's to find out if I truly wanted to teach.

That was my cover story. In fact, I felt crazy again, unable to breathe or concentrate, choking and needing to burst out of the stuffy bowels of the library, and the male domain of the graduate school.

Not giving up, I sought help from psychiatrists at the university infirmary for my debilitatingly terrifying feelings—later to be diagnosed as panic attacks and PTSD flashbacks. As I told the intake doctor of my terrors, I discovered his agenda was to recruit me for their study on student sexuality. Again, I walked out of the infirmary without the help I needed while carrying my mother's curse of insanity.

Was I unable to convey the suffering, I who had learned to manage my image so expertly? Control was not confidence; however, I could not allow myself to fall apart. I would not betray family secrets especially to myself.

This pattern repeated in law school. I asked for help at the university counseling office and did not receive the guidance I so clearly needed.

After three strikes at getting help with this dis-ease no professional took seriously, I sadly accepted that I had inherited my mother's madness. I would do the best I could regardless, secreting away my crazy insides and avoiding triggers that would disable my sanity. Remember, I didn't know about panic attacks or PTSD. I was like a shell-shocked soldier from the battlefield struggling to make something of her life. In my case, the battlefield that was my biological family, had recreated itself inside of me.

You have to keep breaking your heart until it opens.

Rumi

After three years of feeling out-of-place in another male institution, law school, but pushing myself to do well, I graduated, already hired as assistant attorney general in the criminal division of the Maine attorney general's office. Passing the bar exam is the price of admission into the legal profession. As I sat for the two days of the test, I choked as words on the page skittered away again into meaningless black shapes on white paper. Ambushed by PTSD, I fought to answer questions I could barely read. I failed. I proved my father right again. Shame on me.

Joseph Brennan, the attorney general and my boss, had faith in me, reminding me that many admirable lawyers flunked the bar first time around. I passed the second time, so overprepared that no question could fell me. This time I paid the hefty price for the bar preparation course to learn strategies for the test.

MY SECRET LIFE

I survived by living two lives, an outward life of hard work, professionalism and intellect, while pushing down my inside hell of insanity that struck without warning. Demons in the basement climbed the stairs the minute I let down my vigilance.

Those psychological terms: transference (client attracted to therapist) and counter-transference (therapist attracted to client)? In 1975, I had no idea clients (and sometimes therapists) predictably worked their way through a brief infatuation stage to one another before underlying issues, especially boundary issues for incest survivors, could be identified.

I married that therapist connected to the law school from whom I sought help. Boundaries between clients and doctors back in the day were fluid. Studies have since shown some therapists considered sexual relations with clients to be a useful part of therapy. All I knew again, is that this conundrum was my fault. I was to blame. I had trapped myself. I felt so disabled inside that I needed him to be my keeper. In return, I dedicated myself to being his good wife, cheerful, uplifting, loyal, all those things I had done to prevent my father from beating me and my mother from sliding into depression. Incest is a pattern that does not stop torturing us until we walk through the flaming hoops of shame to confront it. For that, we need help.

And so, at thirty-one I stepped into a personal and professional double life. I play-acted being the responsible adult while being held hostage to the terror of having my bleeding child's heart exposed. Here's how it played out.

YOU HANDLE THIS ONE, HOLLY

As a Harvard undergraduate, he walked campus wielding a tomahawk. He wore a Daniel Boone fringed suede jacket with a Davy Crocket fur hat, racoon tail trailing. He insisted the second amendment to the United States Constitution entitled him to bear arms, to protect himself. With a tomahawk.

In law school, he upped the ante by toting a gun. He trod the hallways packing a handgun. The leather jacket and racoon skinned cap had been jettisoned along with the tomahawk. His stance was now more modern. He insisted on the same treatment he had received at Harvard: freedom to practice his constitutionally guaranteed right to bear arms.

The problem was, his classmates grew worried and antsy with "what if's." What if the gun accidentally goes off? What if he decides he needs to use the gun? What if he drops the gun? Their concerns were legitimate.

"You handle this one, Holly," declared the dean.

A small law school, the University of Maine School of Law in Portland, Maine, had only the dean and assistant dean, a registrar and an alumni/ae director in charge of helping third year students find jobs. As assistant dean, responsible for student oversight, I felt the rightness of the dean's directive. I would handle this. This was my job. I would meet the law student with his gun in the third-floor seminar room, the room with the elongated elliptical dark cherry table. My job was to negotiate a way for everyone in the building to feel safe and be safe.

I prepared. Read the cases. Had my references down.

Was ready to listen and to problem solve:

- How can we find a way for everyone to feel safe while honoring your second amendment rights?

- How shall we balance individual rights with the rights of the community?

The student with his gun seated himself at the head of the table. I sat with my back to the closed door with a view of passing traffic on Deering Avenue below.

We talked as if this were a routine gentlemanly conversation. He made his case while I listened. I told him I understood. I did understand. I restated his position and rationale to assure him he had been heard.

I stated my proposition: How can we balance your individual constitutional right with the rights of others around you to feel safe from danger and possible unintended harm?

I do not recall the content of our conversation. I recall my clarity and focus: keep the school safe.

Together, after discussing options, and being careful (on my part) to frame this as a "both...and" not an "either...or" challenge, we came to a reasonable conclusion: he could have his gun close at hand each day while others in the building, particularly his classmates, would not have to be in close proximity to the loaded gun.

I proposed he keep the gun in the safe in the dean's office.

Perhaps the gun resided rent free daily in that office for his full three years. I did not need to know. I knew what I had to accomplish: diffuse the disturbance, co-create a safe environment and treat the individual with respect. We shook hands and took the elevator down together to inform the dean.

I did not know I was repeating my childhood pattern: diffuse the threat, placate the man, stave off violence, operate from my tensed brain, leave my terrified body behind.

POST-TRAUMATIC STRESS

Afterward when I got home, I shook. I, too, felt unsafe in close proximity to a loaded gun. If a hatchet in my father's hand had terrorized me, imagine the threat of a loaded gun. I couldn't even watch violent movies.

At the meeting, I had sat where I always do, close to the door for instant escape. In restaurants, I expand my scope to sit in a corner against the wall so I can compute the distance to exits and monitor movement in the room. Trauma survivors' hypervigilance dies hard. Our brains are frozen in alert mode.

Grandiosity taps me on the shoulder at threatening times like this as well. The dean asked me to handle this. I agreed to handle it. I have served as my family's unsung hero since birth, remaining loyal to and protective of my abusers.

Abused children make excellent trauma nurses and doctors. Abused children make highly proficient EMTs. Abused children take charge of organizations when others cannot. We learned in our non-childhoods how to pass as adults. We learn to appear larger and stronger and braver than we are. We did not surprise ourselves when we succeeded at crisis management. We did, however, not find giving up adrenalin as our drug-of-choice easy.

To this day, with a deadline, I get the work done. Without a deadline, I dawdle. I marvel at the maturity of colleagues who have a plan with goals, objectives and action steps. I create those orderly plans and write the obligatory lists, only to watch them blow away like sea foam. But in a crisis, I'm your woman. This skill I do not doubt in myself. Adult children are rescuers; we cannot bear to be abandoned or to abandon victims.

Facing crises with strength and clarity is a positive trait of trauma survivors. We channel our fear into taking charge, taking constructive action, and staying calm for others. Isn't this what we perfected as children? When my father's anger would boil toward volcanic rage, he was often skillfully distracted by one of his daughters. When my mother would start slipping into her "gone" zone of hellish moaning and wailing, I encouraged her to work with me in her gardens, dance with me to Snooky Lanson's Top Twenty on the radio, or bake a streusel cake with me in the kitchen. My chatter engaged her and perhaps replaced the demonic replays in her head.

Taking charge frees us momentarily of terror. We tell ourselves we are in control. We need to believe we stand a chance of diffusing or even averting disaster. For the moment, we become the healer, not the victim. Our adrenalin rush does not debilitate, if facilitates.

In my work, I have slid into the home plate of crisis management. Talking down a law student with a gun is an early example. As dean of faculty at another university, I took charge immediately when the campus president took off on international ventures. When supplies fail to show up or audio-visual technology fails? No problem: I've got this. An adult child will step in "to save the day." We survived death over and over as children. As adults, no problem. Survival continues to be our way of life.

THE WAGES OF SIN

Four problems tag along like clunking cans tied to a "Just Married" getaway car.

1. Each trauma drains our resiliency batteries. We quake afterwards. Tension held inside feels explosive and demands release.

We discover we are more than exhausted. Our bodies have endured another trauma.

2. We rarely take care of ourselves after the crisis. Or worse, we actively harm our health. Many trauma survivors keep going, keeping busy, never resting. We self-medicate: "I need a drink. Make mine single malt scotch on the rocks. Top shelf." Or devour a meal, especially with sugary foods. Sugar claims our bodies like any other addictive substance.

3. Our expertise at crisis management pushes us away from the planning, visioning and long-term goal setting we need for balance. Our ingrained hypervigilance scans for the next crisis. Our brain's emergency response systems are the opposite of the executive function reflection time we also require. Burnout stalks us confidently.

4. We become intensity-junkies. Relaxing is not possible. As children who didn't live in safe houses, we had to stay alert. As adults, we carry on. We crave intensity, the rush of rescuing others, the "win" of resolving impossible conflicts. Everyday life is boring by comparison. Our smartphone becomes our bed partner.

YOU DECIDE, DAUGHTER

My mother at 87 lies in Corning hospital, felled by her final stroke, this one stomping the sense out of her left side, stealing her ability to form words, making swallowing food impossible. My father rigidly stands beside her, covering up any feeling, watching caregivers come and go, mind calculating. He is deciding not to exercise his health care proxy obligation, not to be the decision-maker my mother had authorized to make her end-of-life choices.

Having heard of her stroke and hospitalization, I had flown in from work in Dallas on the last flight the night before to discover her thrashing body tied down to the bed. Night nurses let me in regardless of the hour.

As if possessed, my mother writhes, moans, moans, writhes. Her body strains to the side, attempts to break the restraints, fails, leans again to the side. I know well my mother's circle of hopelessness.

She is too ravaged by terror for her eyes to land on me, to see that I had come to be with her, to recall me as her comforter. Terrified myself by memories of her moaning, writhing, tortured soul, I take charge. I sit beside her, take her hand and begin my work of calming, soothing her spirit.

It's Holly, Mom. Just flew in from Dallas. I'm sad you are tied down. Let's see how we can make this better. How about I sing you a hymn?

She sees me then. She hears me then singing her beloved evangelical hymns. Her moaning stops for the words.

I cling to the old rugged cross and exchange it one day for a crown.
I come to the garden alone while the dew is still on the roses.
And he walks with me and he talks with me and he tells me I am his own.
Then sings my soul, my Savior God to Thee, how great Thou art. How great Thou art.
Holy, holy, holy Lord God almighty. Early in the morning our song shall rise to thee.

Her circular writhing slows. She finds her pace in the hymns. I make up verses as needed. What matters is she remembers the music. She is at home in those hymns. She calms, her circling eases. Her moans soften into sighs.

When my voice gives out on Baptist and Methodist hymn singing, I tell stories of beloved moments in her life.

Remember we traveled to Washington, DC and stayed at a Girl Scout camp in the country?

Remember the O'Connors at Buttermilk Falls? Every year we would meet so we kids could rush down the natural stone waterfall. You packed a picnic basket with homemade potato salad, macaroni salad, potato chips, packets of cherry Kool-Aid.

Remember your cartwheel in our backyard every spring, mom?

By the time I grow weary of story-telling, I am grateful she is almost sleeping, I call the nurse to ask if my mother could be released from constraints. Witnessing how un-dangerous my mother has become, the nurse nods.

At perhaps three in the morning just before I leave, I pull out a heart-shaped pink opaque glass music box playing the theme from the Titanic: "Near, far, wherever you are, I believe that the heart does go on."

I advise her if she wakes and feels alone to hold the pink music box and recall the song. I tell her I will be just across the street and will see her in the morning. I ask if she could rest. She nods. Her worn out body and soul crave peace.

Staff at the Corning Radisson across the street become my family. I take care of myself by letting them direct me to my king room and soothe me at breakfast. When I again walk across the parkway to my mother's corner room, I find my father not looking at my mother.

He announces in his way that tells me I have no choice: "You decide daughter."

"All right, I will."

Because I already know. My mother was terrified of being

institutionalized. She would rather die than survive as her own mother had, the next patient in line for shock treatment. A disabled wizened body with crazed stick-up hair. Shriveled body with hell flaming behind her eyes. No. My mother would not endure institutionalization. I told my father that was not what she wanted. Nor would she endure a feeding tube. She'd keep pulling it out. I asked him to call my sister to check with her. She agreed.

My decision had a rightness to it. In my mother's clarity of how she did not want to die, she had foretold her desire for her final days.

I didn't even think that my father might have been fearful of bearing the consequences of making this end-of-life decision. The decision not only meant her days were ending, but that my father's Old Testament punishing God would be keeping score. I knew my mother's wishes. Always had. A loving God would not want my mother to suffer.

In my mother's final ten days on earth, she and I experienced "the last great blessing," a time when love is no longer withheld and clarity about that love prevails. My mother had never been able to tell me how she felt about me, so I asked her.

"Mom, was I a good daughter to you?"

Unable to speak, she nodded and squeezed my hand hard.

"Mom, did you think I was attractive?"

Again, she squeezed my hand and nodded hard.

I, too, was able to tell her I loved her, and did not want her to suffer. In her language, I tell her she doesn't have to remain on earth for us. She can go home where she has always wanted to be, together as a family with her mother, her brothers and her sisters.

Louise Riggs Bruner dies on the Fourth of July, 1999, never making it to the Twenty-First-Century.

WHAT TO DO WITH BROKEN THINGS
I think of the trees, and how simply they let go.
⌒ *May Sarton*

Chronic progressive multiple sclerosis is a rapacious disease that sucks vitality from every cell in the body. I know. I witnessed my sister Karen live as best she could with that disease for 24 years.

Resourceful, self-sufficient, and of a practical bent, Karen researched every possible antidote to her illness. She drank cranberry juice to avoid urinary tract infections. She worked out on exercise machines to prolong her muscle tone. She practiced as an attorney for as long as she was able, not giving in to exhaustion or sadness. She was a dedicated attorney who had begun as a PhD home economist.

When she was no longer mobile and her eldest daughter married, Karen insisted on walking down the aisle, buoyed up by strong men on each side of her. We held our breath as her depleted body wobbled and pitched toward collapse. Karen did not collapse until she was returned to her pew.

When Karen moved to assisted living followed by the nursing home, I flew into Ohio for visits. Those visits were sad and scary. To watch my once fit and healthy hard-working sister's identity and energy fade into a crumpled husk was stark enough. To watch her mind fail was horrid. It wasn't just the repeated conversations. That I was used to. It was the paranoia, the susceptibility to scam artists, and the attempt to be in control, regardless, that saddened me.

I didn't know until later that when Karen's clarity went and her thinking became spotty, I was sitting again with my mother in her dementia. Doing my job of cheerleader, telling stories, bringing gifts she would enjoy. After eight years surviving on a feeding tube, Karen could no longer be distracted by steaming eggplant parmesan, her favorite.

We talked as much as talking was possible, we sisters so far apart in memory and beliefs. Karen adored our father. She was his favorite. I did not deify this man who molested and disdained me. Karen did not hold much respect for our mother, blaming her for being the weaker parent, unequal to our kinglike father. Karen never named our mother's mental illness. No one did.

I had often invited Karen to tell me what she wanted, her end-of-life wishes. She avoided answering sometimes. Or, she asked me the same question repeatedly. "What would you do?"

I responded by saying that her desires mattered most. Over the years, piecemeal and with the help of her church friend, Joyce, I got a sense of what Karen wanted: not to be a vegetable.

She wanted to be able to talk. She had lost that. To move about. She had lost that. To care for herself. She could do nothing for herself. To enjoy meals. To read her *Wall Street Journal* daily. To go to church. None of these was possible.

Karen chose Joyce and me as health care proxies, to make those final decisions if she was unable. She became unable. On that day, when pain sliced its way through her body from toes to gut to throat, she looked at me unblinkingly, as if to say: "Now."

Joyce felt it too. Karen no longer wanted to "live" like this. We told the doctor, who agreed, "It has been time for a while now."

When a family member bluntly knifed me (not Joyce) saying, "You are killing Karen," I responded, "I am not afraid."

I wasn't. I knew my sister Karen. I had sat with her, listened to her, heard her and understood what she asked of me.

I knew my sister. I knew my mother. Families are biologically wired to feel for one another. Our mirror neurons, programed to sense feelings of those nearby, resonate. In a family of survivors, I knew. When Karen had previously been diagnosed with MS, I felt ill for days.

Where does love end and codependency begin?

Where does surviving end and living begin?

The accusing family member apologized later for her attack, admitting she was afraid of the Catholic church's condemnation if she supported me.

LIVING ON PURPOSE

I am forty-something with two children I love, discontented in a long-dead marriage doomed from its origin, comfortable but unchallenged in my work, knowing law is not my calling.

I write poetry at three in the morning, after I sing and rock my son to sleep and I am fully awake.

What has become of my dream?

What can I do? Responsible for people, places, things, how can I earn our living?

How can I support my children and me?

What work would I do if I do work I love?

What do I love? What do I like?

What do I want?

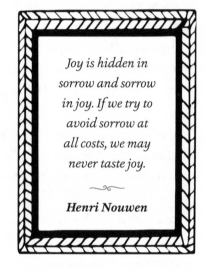

Joy is hidden in sorrow and sorrow in joy. If we try to avoid sorrow at all costs, we may never taste joy.

Henri Nouwen

Raised to be needless and want-less, I flounder on the shore of unknowing. I have crafted a life that allows me to work hard but fails to heal the deep wounds bleeding me white, preventing me from feeling fully alive.

Something is missing.

I recall two questions asked of Peace Corps volunteers returning from foreign assignments, who are preparing to write resumes that will translate their exotic Peace Corps experience into every day marketable skills for American jobs:

- When you felt you were doing what you are meant to do, what were you doing?
- What moments in your life have given you the most joy?

Then came clearly my childhood memory of rain sluicing down the gullies, over the ditches, racing down to the Chemung river. Then came the glee and the bliss and the joy of being on purpose. Being the one who noticed what would free the flow and clear the water's direct pathway. Getting drenched and grassy and sandy? None of that mattered. I was happy and I was unafraid.

Obstacles removed, water flows home to its source.

This removing of obstacles I can do. This clearing the path I can do. This vision of the natural flow of things I feel. This passion to reconnect displaced energy to its source, I feel.

And what do I do with that? How can I support my children and myself on this whimsical desire?

What could I make of that memory that was calling to me so persistently? My life had to change. I had to change. The dis-ease within me had not been healed by dedicating myself to my family, by work successes, by traveling to the fonts of civilization in Europe, by reconciling with my family and again being a dutiful daughter. My soul was dying and without my soul as touchstone for truth, I wouldn't make it.

My parents, who had disowned me for years as a "sinner" because of my unmarried intimate relationship with my first true love, Hank, spoke to me once I became an attorney and decided to marry. Yet, our pretend undiscussed truce gave me no peace. I was living someone else's life and following someone else's dream.

Individual Reflection Questions

—⁓⁓—

1. We are said to be given the same opportunity to learn a lesson as many times as needed until we at last learn what we need to learn. Do the same challenging people keep showing up in your life but with different names and faces? Can you name a dilemma like this you have at last resolved?

2. Have you ever questioned your career choices or your relationship choices, or have you remained contented with those choices? If you have questioned your choices, did you make changes that made things better? Worse? If you did not question your choices, what does that reveal about your core values?

3. Are you a rescuer or a hero at work or in your family? How so? Where do you think you learned that trait? Give an example.

Book Group
Discussion Questions

1. A Buddhist belief suggests we seek two things in life: right work and right relationship. Do you feel you found either one of these? Both? Who do you know that appears to have found both a loving relationship and meaningful work?

2. Have you made the difficult end-of-life decisions such as who will be your health care proxy and how do you want them to determine if it's time for your life to end? Did making those decisions come easily to you or were they troublesome? By what standard would you like your health care proxy to decide if your life is at its end?

3. Do you feel you have unfinished business (unresolved issues) left over from your upbringing? Can you trace those issues back to relationships or events in your youth that never quite got set right? What constructive action could you take now to get help with and heal those issues?

PART 8
Our Painful Past Becomes
our Greatest Asset

*Like all explorers, we are drawn to
discover what's out there without knowing
yet if we have the courage to face it.*

Pema Chödrön

I had to reclaim my life. I had to unearth and live my dream. I had to become a fully alive mother, not controlled by shame and obligation. I had to unleash the goodness inside me to make the difference I was vested at birth with making.

I could no longer be an attorney; I had to be true to my calling. But first, I had to find my calling.

I had given up on finding professional help to stop my internal bleeding from untended childhood wounds. Still terrified of going crazy like my mother and her mother, I was captive to the stalking terror of annihilation inside me. I was faking my life.

Choosing change is deciding to hurt. Loving requires not just courage to risk all things, loving requires surrendering the illusion of "control." When I chose to reclaim my life, I made a blind faith decision to heal. When the man in the row behind me at a chamber music concert said, "My Uncle Herman always said 'love is loss,'" my heart took that in.

The cost was high. I would lose my children, my marriage, Maine friends, financial security, my house, beloved 1930s cottage on a lake in Maine, career and established identity. I would rediscover our world is not always kind to self-defining women.

LOSS UPON LOSS

Yes, I lost my children, a rupture from which we are still healing.

Divorce courts in the 1980s could be adamantly disapproving of women who defied the status quo. Women like me who had pioneered entry into once male professions were reprimanded: *Because you chose a man's career, you will be treated like the man in this divorce settlement. Custody to the father, visitation and school vacations to the working mother, and hefty child support payments by the mother.*

Stunned by the starkness of the decree, my attorney on his own appealed to the supreme judicial court of Maine; I had run out of funds to pay him. The SJC refused to hear the appeal. My world went dark.

For years, I flopped about trying to find my way: taking seasonal work at the post office or being a census worker, to pay child support and bills. Severed from my once successful life in Maine, tripping into relationships with unavailable men who could help me share expenses, I became close to agoraphobic from gripping panic attacks. When my children were with me, I aimed to make our time together as natural, secure, fun and loving for them as possible. This was painful, given our broken hearts.

Blaming myself for losing my children, I was ashamed to tell old friends how deeply I was hurting. At the same time, I quietly and slowly put one foot in front of another to find or create work I was meant to do. My world went dark, my heart ached without ending, my back was broken, yet I refused to quit on myself. The divorce decree was not me. Although it controlled my life, it was not me.

One visit to the gray and grieving women at a Mothers Without Custody meeting woke me up. These shamed and exiled women blamed themselves for acting to reclaim their lives. They lost custody because they too stepped out of the accepted path. They seemed to be accepting a life sentence sequestered in tiny apartments, condemned to unhappiness in order to meet their obligations.

I wish I could show you when you are lonely or in the darkness, the astonishing light of your own being.

Hafiz

Wanting to live our lives and be mothers at the same time, we were not wrong for that choice no matter what the courts said. Women struggle still with the impossibility and consequences of their choice on this.

I grieve now, recalling those years. I am grateful to have forged and maintained a loving and honest relationship with my son, who chose to live with me as soon as he was able. By being his mom, I have come to believe unconditional love is possible, essential and magnificent.

For the loss of my daughter, I grieve. For the loss of my daughter, my heart aches. I know what not having a mother is like. I will always love my daughter.

STEPPING OUT INTO THE LIGHT

My earliest memory is of light. Pure, glowing, welcoming, gentle white light. I recall a tunnel of light, opening to unbridled light. The radiance was at once inside and outside of me. The light and I were not separate. I trust this vivid visceral memory.

When I was two, I sat myself on an anthill to witness the busy intentional energies of those tiny beings. I don't believe I hurt them. Not one of the ants bit me. I imagined they welcomed me and my fascination with them and their industriousness.

One sister and I were separately exploring the back yard of our Fourth Street apartment on "Irish Hill" in Corning. Possibly my sister noticed what I was doing and ordered me to move while I, contented, chose to stay with my busy friends. That sister likely stole inside to tell our mother, at work scrubbing her kitchen. Our mother was forever scrubbing something.

A wailing force shaped like my mother burst out the door at me, crazed and shrieking. She snatched me off the sandy mound, shook me and stood me under the spigot of the deep kitchen sink.

I did not fathom her actions. The moment before, I was welcomed to a charming small creatures' parade. The light felt soft and clear like a halo around me.

Of a sudden, I was captive in a desperate large animal's cage. What message does a baby girl take away from that experience? I grieve for my mother. She tried to save her baby from harm, instead terrorizing as she had been terrorized.

I love you, mom. You tried so hard to find your sanity. I know you loved me in your own way.

May I tell you how I found the halo of light again?

MY DAY BACK IN COURT

Today I went to court as defendant, *pro se* (my own advocate), I did not expect to prevail. My goal: do my best and let go of the outcome. The Serenity Prayer's message, right? Change what I can and let go of the rest.

My velocity, seventy-five in a fifty-five zone along Route 2 traveling west through Massachusetts. I wasn't paying attention. Delayed flights home the night before led to my 2:00 a.m. landing in Manchester, New Hampshire, with an additional hour's drive ahead of me.

On four flimsy hours of sleep, I got up, showered, stepped back behind the wheel and headed to my appointment in Brattleboro, Vermont. Too weary to concentrate, intent on reaching Brattleboro in time, I mused as I drove, witnessing cars pass me by.

When the state trooper with blue flashing lights neared, I thought: *he's coming for some guy up ahead that passed me.*

Clean driving records scrub down automobile insurance costs. My record until this moment was clean. No extra points to drive my premium up.

Fear of authority figures and the need to "people please" will leave us.

~

Promise 4,
Adult Children of Alcoholics (ACA) Promises

This has not always been the case. Five years ago, I participated in "Bad Girls' School," the punitive full day remediation program for Massachusetts drivers who have "earned" more points on their driver's license than allowed by state law. That Day of Shame put me in such a tizzy, I vowed never again to mess up.

I messed up. By not paying attention, I committed a traffic violation. When the state trooper told me my speed, I felt awful and spoke my heartfelt apology. Not only was my speed unsafe, I wasn't even aware I was speeding. I acknowledged how bad I felt. Owned that my speed could have led to harm. Admitted I was troubled about the increase in car insurance this would cost.

I was struck but not flattened by a slam-bam shame attack. I had not relapsed into Bad Girl "shame on me, I am a pig for a daughter" self-abuse. This gentler response felt new and ever so welcome. I had made a mistake; but, that no longer meant I am a mistake.

The police officer suggested I talk with the judge. That surprised me. Traffic court is, I thought, *pro forma.* Law broken. Case over.

My "listen to what he is saying" inner ear cocked to the side.

"Okay, officer. You're right. Why not? What do I have to lose?"

My well-honed fear of authority figures and authority counter-dependence lightened their grip on me. I appealed.

Months later, I entered the district courtroom. The judge magistrate acknowledged me standing alone as the state trooper seated beside him ripped through the rap sheet at the speed of reading the warnings in a drug commercial. I asked if he could slow down so I could process his words. The judge magistrate motioned for me to speak.

"Your honor, I have two things to offer:

1. *I make an amend for this, have learned my lesson and changed my behavior.*

2. *I ask that you consider an alternate consequence to a fine and points on my license. I request a form of community service. I would be grateful to be of service in a police station or to read stories to children at Head Start."*

The judge magistrate drew a circle with his pen on my summons then a slash through the circle. Turning to the trooper, the magistrate smiled.

"She must have sweet talked Officer Jablonski."

"Sweet talked? No, sir, I told the truth. I felt awful."

The trooper beckoned me forward.

"Think you can get the judge to color his hair like you do? That purple is awesome."

Not missing a beat, I responded, "Sure, with his white hair, the judge would rock this style.

> *Instead of standing on the shore and proving to ourselves that the ocean cannot carry us, let us venture on its waters just to see.*
>
> **Pierre Teilhard de Chardin**

But with your dark hair, you'd need to go with a thunder bolt cut-out like David Ortiz."

We belly laughed together.

Judge pronounced, "You are free. No fee. No penalty."

I went to court an assumed-guilty defendant, and emerged wondering what happened? Did I just experience a spirit-of-the-law exception prevail over a letter-of-the law judgment? Did something miraculous just happen? Did I face my fear of authority without caving to shame or puffing myself up into defensive grandiosity?

The noon sky was gloriously clear. So enchanted was I by this unexpected gift, I had to turn myself around and walk back into the foyer to make sure I had heard what I had heard: Innocent! *No charge. Free.*

Now comes the innocent. Spring birds outside announce with trumpeting calls: *Now comes the innocent.*

Innocent.

ASKING FOR AND ACCEPTING HELP

I had not learned to ask for help. As a child, I was expected to know how to do things without seeking guidance. Asking for help led to scorn. Disdain was my father's punishment: "You ought to be ashamed of yourself. Can't you get anything right?" On my own, I observed and studied and practiced until I wouldn't fail at tying my shoes, writing letters of the alphabet, or taking my turn at the forward roll.

As a four-year-old in first grade, I had no choice but to master every lesson. If I failed to keep up, I would be sent home to take care of my troubled mother, frightening as that often was. If I was sick and missed a class, I would panic until I could catch up to Mrs. McClure's lesson.

Failure was not an option. My first academic panic attack (or full-blown PTSD flashback) befell me when Mrs. McClure asked me a question I could not answer, because I had missed class the day before. I determined to learn from classmates what I had missed in class so as to never be vulnerable again.

When I sought help at university with panic attacks, I was at best rebuffed by counselors and at worst, taken advantage of in my vulnerability. Asking for help was too high a risk.

After years of floundering, looking to inappropriate (primarily emotionally unavailable) people for assistance, I "bottomed out." In everyday terms, bottoming out is becoming sick and tired of being sick and tired. When I keep repeating the same mistakes, I know I am at the bottom.

Isolating myself was not helping. I turned to confront my fears of intimacy and vulnerability face to face. Of people I respected, I asked, "Do you know a truly competent therapist, especially someone who is trauma-savvy?" Once I had my short list, I interviewed therapists boldly and authentically. When my list got down to two, I trusted my intuition and selected the decidedly more seasoned counselor, Dr. Bernard Gray.

Once I began to talk, I did not stop. My dysfunction felt bottomless; my determination to heal was equally endless. I was getting the help I had needed forever and I wasn't going to blow it! What a mess I was! My fearless, competent, humorous image cracked. My honesty terrified me. My misplaced loyalty to my family's dysfunction exhausted me. My facility at harming myself emotionally saddened me. Memories seared my heart. Twice a week I showed up, determined to ask for, accept and use the help even when I felt it was killing me. In fact, the false part of me was dying; but, without it, I had little protection.

I challenged Dr. Gray. I fought him. I idealized him. I was attracted to him. Oh Lord, not again! This time, I was aware of transference and was not saddled by any counter transference.

I had met a professional whose respect I could feel. I was at last heard, and for the first time, understood.

Trauma survivors are dying to be heard. We ache to be taken seriously, to be understood. When we at last find our listener, our lives begin.

I had chosen him. At last I was making healthy choices. I was climbing over another hilltop. Even my work was getting clearer. Readers of my books and articles sought me out to tell me my honesty had helped them face their fears and also, to seek help.

> *Fears of failure and success will leave us as we*
> *intuitively make healthier choices.*
> *⌒ **ACA Promise #10***

My international and stateside keynotes and team-building sessions became compelling. I don't advertise; I rely on word of mouth. Word was getting out and speaking invitations were abundant.

When I keynote, I rarely lecture or see myself as an expert. Instead, I engage with participants, inviting them to share, listening to them, building on their wisdom. Participants and I co-create safe spaces where truth can be told with love and strategies created to make things

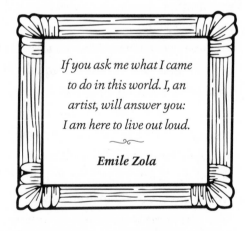

If you ask me what I came to do in this world. I, an artist, will answer you: I am here to live out loud.

Emile Zola

better. I began to feel as at home with 2,000 people as with two.

Asking the right people for help and accepting that help are miraculous for me, as is my choice of work. I support and challenge early childhood professionals, especially leaders, to hone and trust their genius despite public disparagement as "glorified babysitters." I support people who make a difference.

Change the life of a child and you change the world. Little Hollywog reclaimed her voice that was beaten out of her. As she spoke her truth, others stepped out more and more to speak their truths. I spoke in India, Macau, Iceland, Hungary, New Zealand, northern Manitoba, Singapore. In the end heartfelt connection is what matters. The more vulnerable I became, the stronger my voice grew.

TAKING IT TO THE LAUNDROMAT

Having come to trust my counselor, I wanted to learn to entrust my peers with my vulnerability. My go-to defense had always been to appear confident and competent aka invulnerable. We Bruner girls were adept image managers. That image I had painstakingly constructed to survive no longer served me. In fact, my image was isolating me.

I choose two dear friends, one female and one male, to serve as my co-sponsors. Co-sponsors are wounded fellow travelers (trauma survivors) equally passionate about healing with help from trauma-informed literature, people and practices.

Nina and Ted have my back every day and night as needed. We check in on one another via *WhatsApp* any time. We stay true to ourselves by sharing our truths with love.

Your heart and my heart are very, very old friends.
⌒ Hafiz

We do not waste time judging ourselves or each other. When I am hurting, I ask for help. When I am happy, I share my joy.

When I start to isolate, I level with them. When I don't like myself, I ask for feedback about my strengths. When I can't see my way through to the other side of a block, I have friends to sit with me and hold my hand.

I accept what they say because it is true for them. When asked for my opinion, I offer what I am learning on the same issues they are facing: feeling abandoned, blaming myself, not trusting, losing self-confidence, feeling hopeless. I am no one's savior, however I offer my experience, my lessons learned, my strengths honed through adversity, and always hope. They in turn choose what they want from what I offer. I trust their choices and their timing. I do not measure myself by whether I have had an impact. Instead, I ask myself: am I loving?

That's what trauma-surviving fellow travelers do. We three seekers accept each other. We support. We love. We love one another. Like three puppies, we love unconditionally.

Three wounded people practicing kind-heartedness. Three wounded people applauding one another's small steps toward dignity. Three wounded people supporting one another when our confidence wanes and we slip into self-blame or, ever more troubling, self-hatred. Yes to:

- Asking for help

- Accepting help

- Speaking the unspeakable, the taboo, the secrets that could have killed my spirit

- Opening to sunlight

- Trusting darkness precedes light

- Co-creating and carefully tending our families of choice

- Not having to be perfect, "have it together" or puff up into grandiosity

- Choosing not to dissociate or to self-medicate with drugs of choice like sugar, the internet or television

- Reclaiming my soul, the soul that arched its way out of my collapsing body before I lost consciousness after one of my father's beatings

- Welcoming my soul home

This soulful connection with fellow travelers, like time with my trusted counselor, saves me. Isolating is no longer my first desire. Connecting is. Sharing pains along with gains. Sharing our truths sustains all three of us.

Ted named us the Laundromat. After all, we bring our dirty laundry to wash out and get help folding our

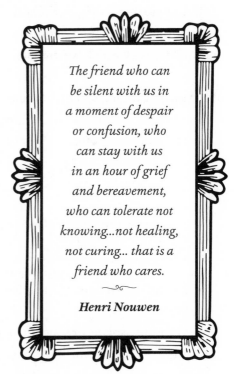

The friend who can be silent with us in a moment of despair or confusion, who can stay with us in an hour of grief and bereavement, who can tolerate not knowing...not healing, not curing... that is a friend who cares.

Henri Nouwen

clean sheets. In our laundry baskets we bring soiled linens, smudged and dirty cottons, rayon and hemp, even resilient bamboo, all for cleansing. We unload them all into the washers at the Laundromat.

I have learned from my Laundromat friends neither to fear nor withhold. I marvel as Nina tells stories of having been an angry young mother. I sit fixated as Ted quietly describes a resentment he is releasing. I open up about my worries, self-doubts, and fear paralysis. I listen to discern when to let go, when to step up.

CHOSEN FAMILIES, NEW GROUND RULES

We need a tribe. We, the outliers from our families, need a tribe to call our own. We have been "the other" Simone de Beauvoir spoke of: the stranger neither seen nor understood. The unwelcomed one.

In our created tribes, our "chosen families," we can try out, fail, learn from, establish and continuously refine the principles and ground rules by which we interact.

In the Laundromat, we aim not to:

- Make others wrong

- Blame, shame or inflame anyone, including ourselves

- Dissociate, instead to call ourselves home when we abandon ourselves

- Fear the truth or lie to ourselves

- Hide out, isolate, or separate ourselves especially when we feel unworthy

We choose instead to:

- Aim for all our actions and decisions to come from love

- Allow ourselves to feel and let our feelings inform us

  - *I'm antsy: What am I avoiding?*

  - *I'm lonely: I need to reach out.*

  - *I'm angry: How does today's slight land me back in the dark pantry of my childhood?*

- Own our mistakes, learn from them; apologize when appropriate, and change our behavior

- Laugh more spontaneously. *Silly me,* I say. *I forgot that appointment.* (Rather than, *Stupid me, I screwed up again.*)

- Be with folk who love us and challenge us

- Walk away from the company of folk who shame and belittle our souls

These learnings I value soulfully. I trust my friends, my fellow travelers to work with me to keep the water flowing, not stagnating. If dynamics stagnate, we talk about it. What's troubling us? What do we not want to talk about? What would help us get clear again?

Forty years ago, I wrote a similar contract with my husband. He and I were both play-acting at marriage. We acted as we had learned, repeating what was modeled for us. Today, I understand

I have choices. I can't go wrong by being authentic and by inviting others to be true to themselves. When I mess up or fall into blind spots, I can learn. I can recover and I don't have to heal alone.

> *With help from our ACA support group, we will*
> *slowly release our dysfunctional behaviors.*
> ⌒ *ACA Promise #11*

Support groups for trauma survivors meet weekly. We gather to read trauma-informed literature, to share our stories. We tell and we hear the truth. In time, we mature. I have come to trust that my maturing and healing are both intimately linked to the efforts of other trauma-survivors to grow and to heal. Survivor groups have healing powers that undo the damage done by troubled family groups.

SETTING A PRECEDENT FOR HEALING

Both parents alcoholics, his mother killed, his uncle suiciding while babysitting for him, Tony A. knew trauma. Both parents attempted to self-medicate their pain with drinking. Tony tried the same drug. It didn't work.

He found his way to get help "putting down the drink" in Alcoholics Anonymous. He came to see that alcohol and other substance addictions like cocaine or heroin boot us into oblivion, they do not heal. He came to see that process addictions like over-work, piling on accomplishments, posing as "all things to all people," taking charge, attempting to control outcomes, nursing resentments, none of these healed him.

Under pressure to articulate what helps traumatized adult children of dysfunctional families restore our identities and our souls, Tony wrote his version of the traditional Alcoholics Anonymous twelve steps of recovery for Adult Children of Alcoholics (dysfunctional families). In his steps, Tony set aside self-blame for self-acceptance. He viewed defects of character as understandable survival traits we could translate into strengths. Distrust for authority figures could become honest questioning rather than passive aggressive insubordination. People-pleasing to diffuse a potentially dangerous person could be translated into straightforward advocacy, and the confidence to believe our own voice.

With these steps Tony offered, we could unlearn unhealthy practices and learn to love, forgive and trust. For those of us whose family dysfunction did not include alcoholism, we substitute our truth: we admit we are powerless over living with the trauma of dysfunction.

Take a look; do these steps have any relevance to you? If you have read the original twelve steps, you will see the differences. Tony's steps are about learning how to love, forgive and trust.

1. We admitted we were powerless over the effects of living with alcoholism (family dysfunction) and that our lives had become unmanageable.

2. We came to believe that a power greater than ourselves could bring us to clarity.

3. We made a decision to practice self-love and to trust a Higher Power of our understanding.

4. We made a searching and blameless inventory of our parents because in essence we had become them.

5. We admitted to our Higher Power, to ourselves and another human being, the exact nature of our childhood abandonment.

6. We were entirely ready to begin the healing process with the aid of our Higher Power.

7. We humbly asked our Higher Power to help us with the healing process.

8. We became willing to open ourselves to receive the unconditional love of our Higher Power.

9. We became willing to accept our own unconditional love by understanding that our Higher Power loves us unconditionally.

10. We continued to take personal inventory and to love and approve of ourselves.

11. We sought through prayer and meditation to improve our conscious contact with our Higher Power, praying only for knowledge of its will for us and the power to carry it out.

12. We have had a spiritual awakening as a result of taking these steps, and we continue to love ourselves and to practice these principles in all our affairs.

Tony's message to me? *Become willing to accept unconditional love. Believe I am worthy of love. Dare to accept my "as is" self.*

Learn to love myself first. When I can love myself, rather than degrade myself as I had learned, I can make a difference. Not an easy task, but freeing.

> *The heart is made of the same*
> *substance as the heavens.*
> ⌇ **Hong Zicheng**

Individual Reflection Questions

1. Does your family have written ground rules for how to interact with one another? Most families have unwritten ground rules which everyone is expected to grasp and to follow. If you were to write out your family's unwritten ground rules, what would you write? For example, is being on time an unwritten rule? To whom must respect be given? What are the consequences for disrespect?

2. Have you sought help on personal/professional difficulties from someone beyond your family? How did that work out? What made that relationship productive or what caused it to fail? Is there someone in your family whom you trust to help you work through challenges? How does that work for you?

3. What sense do you make of Pema Chödrön's claim: "Like all explorers, we are drawn to discover what's out there without knowing yet if we have all the courage to face it." Have you taken a risk to change something about your life/work without knowing if you could follow through on whatever happened?

Book Group
Discussion Questions

1. How do you feel when twelve step groups such as Alcoholics Anonymous are mentioned? Are those groups for addicts who need them only and have no relevance to you? If you, like the author, substitute "dysfunctional family" for "alcoholism," do any of Tony's twelve steps above apply to you?

2. Have you ever formed a group with other people and developed ground rules for how that group will conduct itself? What ground rules worked? Which ones caused dissension? What helps a group succeed rather than fall apart?

3. How easy or difficult for you is trusting others with intimate details of your life challenges? How do you determine who is trustworthy and who is not? What do you do to keep that relationship honest and vital? Have you been able to learn from a betrayal by a trusted person, or do you hold a resentment toward the person?

PART 9

Trauma Survivor
Seeks Deeper Source

*Every positive change—every jump to a higher level
of energy and awareness—involves a rite of passage.*

*Each time to ascend to a higher rung on the ladder
of personal evolution, we must go through a
period of discomfort, of initiation.*

I have never found an exception.

Dan Millman

To reclaim myself from the trauma I survived, I have tried different pathways to connect with something holy, something sacred. Some pathways work. Some do not. I keep learning.

For a long time, I wanted to know who God is. More precisely, I desired a loving relationship with the divine, if there was a divine. Just as Hollywog dug for Jacob's ladder, and rolled toward the pearly gates, I haven't given up on aligning with a divine force of healing love.

As I share below my discoveries from my efforts, I will also share new ways of seeing old stories. The "cover story" I had repeated to myself became infused with new and deeper meaning as I learned to trust my heart.

I am still seeking, and I accept I may always be. Nonetheless, I remain enthusiastically open to the possibility of a higher power, to God, to that spiritual source of goodness.

If you find my stories somewhat disjointed, trust yourself. They are as disjointed as they came to me. I am able to recall painful experiences only when I have gained enough understanding to face and grieve these experiences.

Survivors' stories, as Dr. van der Kolk reminds us, do not come with neatly shaped beginnings, middles and ends.

YOU ARE WITH ME ALWAYS

I am happy for people who have a god with a face and a name, a god whom they feel unconditionally loves them. I am enthusiastically open to the possibility of a relationship like that to a loving God. I have not given up Hollywog's search for Jacob's ladder.

In a meditation session, I visualized myself as a child. I invited this child, this Hollywog, to share with me any secret or memory she was comfortable sharing. If she didn't feel like sharing, that was okay, too.

I assured her I would listen either way. I wanted particularly to recall memories of experiences I had hidden from myself. I hoped I was at last ready to accept and grieve those experiences.

I breathed in and out as I waited. I jettisoned thoughts such as, "What am I cooking for dinner," and "Do I need to return anyone's call?" as they flew through my consciousness. I breathed deliberately again.

Hollywog's persistence got my attention. I observed her as she stomped her feet, angrily demanding of the divine.

Where are you, she demanded. WHERE ARE YOU?

I need a hug.

I need to be rocked. To be soothed. To be comforted.

I want to feel loved.

Where are you? I need you now!

I'm tired of waiting for you.

God of the gender-free voice responded, *You are with me always.*

What? I am with you always. Come on! What good is that if I cannot feel you hug me?

To conclude the stuck meditation, I soothed the brave and hurting little girl. I thanked her for asking the tough question, hugged her for asking for what she needed.

Quietly, I reflected on that minor spatial change. This god didn't say, "I am with you always." This god said, "You are with me always."

Now what do I do with that? I learn to love the question.

THIS BUSINESSMAN GOD IN A PALE KHAKI SUIT

Meditation can include visualizations, often guided, sometimes not. On my recovery quest to build a relationship with a loving spiritual source, I invited this source unseen to join me as I meditated.

As often happens, who I was as a little girl, the feisty scrapper "Hollywog" showed up to represent me again.

With my eyes closed, I watched Hollywog march directly up to a man of average build in a 1950s style military brush cut, sporting a khaki business suit.

Hollywog, feisty four-year-old me was hopping mad at this man who said he was God.

She got up in his face, stomped her feet and demanded he answer her:

How could you allow atrocities to happen to children?

How can you allow babies to be abused, beaten, molested, not fed, not hugged?

Do you know how long it takes us to recover?

Do you know the work it takes to feel sane?

Do you see how many of us don't make it?

How can you allow open-hearted little children with no defenses to suffer?

Some of us never find our way home. Some of us suicide. How can you allow this?

Where is your "unconditional love" for these babies? Where? You tell me now!

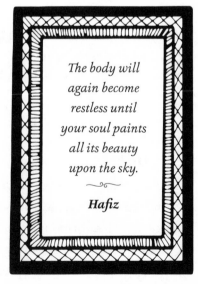

The body will again become restless until your soul paints all its beauty upon the sky.

Hafiz

Hollywog wagged her index finger in the man-god's face.

This god appeared surprised and delighted by Hollywog's passionate stance This god smiled in appreciative amazement.

Hollywog was not going to let this god off. She stayed up there. Up in his face, demanding how he could allow this cruelty, this acid splashed on the hearts of innocents. This god looked at this outraged sputtering articulate little girl and sighed.

Design defect. It was a design defect.

In my dream, this god made Hollywog laugh with him and at the pain and at herself.

Without explanation, both Hollywog and I felt relieved. Perhaps the god-man did too. He smiled.

Now what was that about? Who is this god who makes mistakes and admits them?

DO WORK THAT ENHANCES THE SOUL

Terrified. Fried. Wired. Jumpy. I jogged down the sidewalks in my Inman Square neighborhood in Cambridge, hoping exercising would lessen my stress.

Almost agoraphobic in my pain, I wouldn't run far from the sanctuary of my 700-square-foot condominium. End of my rope. No paid work. No longer an attorney. Terrified of not being able to sustain my children's needs. Alone. Frantic. I demanded to know, "What can I do?"

God of the gender-free clear nonjudgmental voice again spoke.

"Get out of your current financial crisis. Then do work that enhances the soul."

I stopped running, literally. Something in these words was real. Just as I knew Principal Bebout was saving my four-year-old life by letting me catapult into first grade, I felt these words offered the guidance I was missing.

Do work that enhances the soul.

This response bore a rightness. If I aligned my life metaphorically with the work of clearing channels for water to flow to the sea, I would live "on purpose."

How could I earn a living by aligning myself with some deep and natural flow? I would ask for help to find my way.

WE CAN'T BE HAPPY AND YOU CAN'T BE HAPPY EITHER

Centering prayer is another form of meditation I tried. *Read a passage. Listen for the word that calls you. What image appears when you hear that word? Place yourself there. Feel your surroundings. Be still.*

One morning in my Cambridge condo's petite living room that was also a dining room, I meditated asking my inner child to share something she had experienced that I was blocking from memory.

I waited. Waited. Almost nodded off. I didn't know then that traumatic memories return only when we have built the emotional strength and support systems to face those ruptures.

Hollywog walked silently up to me, inviting me to lean my ear toward her, this little girl in the white smocked dress with the lace unraveling from the right sleeve. I remembered that hand-me-down dress. She motioned me closer to whisper a secret.

I held still. At last I would learn what happened. She would tell me what I have repressed. She knows. I breathed in and breathed out, imagining I was ready to hear and accept.

She steepled her hands over her mouth so she could safely whisper the secret of my family, likely for centuries.

We can't be happy and you can't be happy either.

The cost of being accepted by those Bruno and Riggs tribes? Perpetual loyalty to unhappiness. Doomed soul. Joy an illusion.

We can't be happy. Happy? Joyous? Free?

Never. Not allowed.

I was stung by her secret. Damn, I wanted details, intact memories returned! What happened that broke my spirit and choked my heart? What drove us to zombiehood?

Slowly, I began to understand the power and exactitude of her sharing that family command with me.

She had shared the legacy I inherited and in part, passed on to my own children: Life is about hard work and accomplishment, not about joy.

I determined to step outside the family legacy and no longer stay loyal to this secret command.

PLANTING MY FEET

I hold this belief: as an educator, I want to live what I teach. My mother, a woman of slogans, stressed: *Practice what you preach.* I believe each child and every adult deserves to be respected, listened to and appreciated for her or himself.

While holding myself to this worthy standard of authenticity, I confounded my vision with something dark and un-seeable: perfectionism fueled by terror. Perfectionism was a cover for my feeling unworthy and inadequate. I feared people would see my flaws and fire me. Darker still, I pushed down secrets I hid from myself about my uneasy history.

Obeying the "Don't talk, don't trust, don't feel" unwritten troubled family rule, I acted as if everything were hunky-dory in my family. Don't educators need to represent healthy families while setting a good example? Given that my childhood was unhealthy, how could I be a healthy teacher?

Brave called my bluff of all places in the midst of presenting one of my earliest keynotes (translated into Vietnamese) in Boston. Sharing research on children and abuse, I flashed back to (pictured) myself as a child passing out during a violent beating by a father's fists. That unbidden ghost-memory clutched my throat until I could not breathe, speak, nor stop tears tsunami'ing toward my eyes.

Run! I wanted (as I had as child) to run screaming for the hills.

"Shut up!" the abuser yelled at the little child inside me, flash-freezing her into a pillar of ice. Chilled, terrified I would faint, I felt shame threatening to flush me off that stage and out of my livelihood!

With extraordinary inexplicableness, my heart became my voice. I stopped holding my breath and planted my feet on the floor to notice where I was.

In that wobbly moment, I determined I must tell my truth: I was sexually, physically, emotionally and spiritually abused throughout my childhood. I had kept silent out of loyalty to my family. I was the statistic I was talking about in my keynote.

From my heart then, I thanked each early childhood professional for her/his life-giving role in helping children like me feel safe, protected, cared for and yes, loved. I described how Michael Gonta, my first teacher, valued me and provided my first sanctuary for learning: "Without teachers like you and Mr. Gonta, I wouldn't be standing here today," I marveled.

We will discover our real identities by
loving and accepting ourselves.
ACA Promise #1

I then interlaced my story as a survivor with the research, wrapping my keynote with enough clarity and ample conviction. Applause beamed light on my truth-telling path waiting to unfurl before me.

To speak up for wounded children, I claimed my truest voice. My greatest vulnerability became my greatest strength. I discovered I could stand up for children with invisibly bleeding wounds. Since that moment, I have spoken for survivors because, as Diana Nyad says, "Freedom lies in being bold."

UPON MEETING HER GRANDSON

My mother's first words when she met my ten-month-old son who had just arrived from Korea: "I hope no one abuses him."

MEMORIES FLY HOME TO ME,
PORTENDING DEEPER MEANING

Bubbling over with champagne'd excitement, so many stories to tell about my first semester away at the women's college, I dutifully report to my father as he sits in his recliner throne in the music room. Reporting on my courses, I recall another learning. The senior women have taken us first year women to New York City's Greenwich Village to help us learn to handle ourselves wisely in the city.

Bustling towards us in a bevy of glitter and pizzazz, bedecked with royal blue eye shadow, long eyelashes, coiling honeyed hair. Dazzling in the night. Their hot pink feather boas flicking like perturbed cats' tails. Their pizzazz. Their freedom. These (perhaps) men strutting freedom. I do not judge beyond that, because I am gobsmacked by their freedom to express themselves.

I had witnessed my first men in drag, I would later learn. Mrs. Doubtfire and Tootsie had yet to cross my path in Corning, New York. These spritely folk enchanted me.

"You didn't see that, daughter," commands my father, rising over me to his full height.

I know his words hold a message that will help me later when I am ready. Ready to accept I was raised by a father who believed he could dictate my thinking. Inject his way inside my thoughts to excise unacceptable thinking.

"You didn't see that daughter."

How many other moments did he command I forget, not believe my own eyes, not honor my soul's way of knowing? Insanity is planted in these commands.

THE GRANDFATHER I WAS NOT ALLOWED TO KNOW

I didn't know any of my grandparents, which was curious because they were so important to my mother and father. At last, my mother and I made a trip to Sodus, New York, to my grandfather's old farm, where he had a horse I was promised I could ride. Hoisted up on the horse's back, led around the small corral, then pulled down!

No fair! I wanted to hold the reins and ride that horse on my own.

Disillusioned, I wandered around the farm on my own, looking for something of interest. A man in khakis, who must have been my grandfather, came down off his porch offering me something. He held out a chocolate Easter bunny, so old it had turned mostly white. He said I could have the Easter bunny if I went inside his house with him. I was curious, if not trusting.

Lightning bolt ripped down from the sky! Aunt Esther sputtered as she rushed in to snatch away the expired chocolate my grandfather Orma John was using to lure me inside his darkly curtained farmhouse.

"Don't take that," Esther commanded as she pushed me away from him and the allure of the chocolate Easter bunny.

No grandparent had ever noticed me. I was surprised he had sought me out and offered to give me something. I did not understand Esther's sharp intervention. I was fascinated, even mesmerized, by getting to be with this grandfather who seemed interested in me.

I sensed the gravity of her action. In my child's heart, I noted something important had just transpired. I knew in her brusque way, Aunt Esther had saved me. I wondered, what was the danger? After all, he was my grandfather. He was a grandfather offering a little girl, his granddaughter, candy.

Abuse runs in families until one person stops running from the truth.

The vacant look in my mother's eye when she left her body.

Her ungodly moans in the night, growing so out of control, I hear my father opening the front door to a doctor who climbs the stairs with his black bag. The doctor injects my mother with something. Her bellowing stops.

Aunt Olive sputtering how she hated her father. *I hated that man!*

Me choking at night, terrified of the demanding man standing over me, forcing me to do things unspeakable.

Pedophile. For months, I quaked as I mouthed that forbidden word to describe my own father. Had my mother endured the same sexual abuse with her father I had with mine? No one is left to tell.

WE DON'T TALK ABOUT THAT

A male cousin lays down the non-negotiable law, "We don't talk about that," as I invite him and other male cousins to level about the whispered but powerful report that another cousin had molested his daughter.

We sit together on couches. I am the only female cousin in the room. The women are perhaps attending to the meal or the children? Red wine has been poured generously. We had appeared to be sharing from the heart, the conversation affable.

With an equally intentional voice I say, "Truth sets me free. Even if others don't talk about it, I talk about the abuse I experienced. Talking out these difficult things helps me heal. *These secrets can otherwise kill us.*"

In the immediate weighted descent of silence, glasses are topped off with blood red Cabernet Sauvignon. Do not talk. *Do not trust. Do not feel.* Dr. Claudia Black observes these are the unspoken ground rules of traumatized families. If we don't talk about it, it didn't happen.

Later on, in another room, a woman who married into the family confirms the father-daughter molestation and the divorce by his wife that resulted. This, in a family where divorce was forbidden.

I hear indirectly other claims of father-daughter abuse.

I reach out to the ex-wife of the cousin accused of molesting their daughter, suggesting we might have coffee and share our stories and what we have learned so far in our lives. Guillotine descends. Slams down a rageful blade. Connection forever severed.

In sadness, I trust my instincts. Being alone in speaking the truth severs me from family circles. I am not invited back. I will find my way home to my own family, a circle where truth-telling with love unites us.

I AM MY FATHER'S KEEPER

The childhood journals my mother stacked and saved for me sit alongside my near-bald teddy bear, Growly; my pogo stick; and my red, trimmed-with-gold, cowgirl's shirt. I open the red journal and begin to read again the record of my early elementary school days.

I come to the section where I warned my father that I would leave because *hurting me isn't right* and he responded, *Don't leave; I couldn't live without you daughter.*

I understand how, after that, I feel responsible for keeping my father alive. I become my father's keeper in addition to being my mother's caregiver.

DEPRESSION ERA FATHERLESS FAMILY

When I tell my uncle Buster about my mother's mental illness, he dismisses my words. His wife Loretta stops him, commanding, "You need to listen to her, Bus."

He is anxious and unable to listen as I describe mother's jagged psychotic episodes.

At a family reunion, my cousin offers a butterscotch beige teaspoonful of condensed milk, boiled down to a sweet sticky caramel, for us to taste. She tells us, "This is the only treat our parents had growing up. They all shared one spoon and passed it around."

When I ask my mother why she feels so attached still to her mother, she answers, "She kept us all together."

The threat of poor farms, the foster system, homelessness. My grandmother in her insanity at least kept her eight children with her. They never separated from her emotionally or spiritually. She inhabited them.

WOMEN AND MADNESS

When my mother said, "I'm going home," she meant to her mother's home. Her mother's by then was an added-on room at uncle James' house, where my grandmother rocked in angry vacantness, the vacantness of a woman who endured shock treatments with a stick in her mouth to keep her from swallowing her tongue.

This same stern Calvinist evangelical woman, my grandmother, was the daughter of a Jewish woman, surname Schultz, descended from the Bavarian Schimmelhorns. My mother tells me this only after I marry a Jewish man. She has kept her family's secret. Now I understand why mother's rants in German sounded Yiddish. Her guttural explosions translated: *You are a jackass. What do I have, pigs for daughters?* My mother repeated what she had heard. She primarily spoke in clichés and handed-down invectives. Like me, no one had asked her to speak for herself.

How on earth had this Jewish grandmother morphed into a zealous born-again Christian? What caused her to abandon her own heritage and faith? What real or metaphorical pogroms haunted her past? Her untold history, did it manifest in her confinement in a state insane asylum?

If the theory is correct and trauma is inherited, passed on to us epigenetically, what a heritage of women and loss, women and insanity is passed down to me.

> *You may learn as I did, that many of these*
> *patterns don't belong to us; they've merely been*
> *borrowed from others in our family history.*
> ⌒ **Mark Wolynn**, It Didn't Start with You

No wonder I felt cursed, almost as if I had the "mark of the devil" on my brain. The suffocating weight on my chest was generations of trapped women who had no choice but to submit to men who felt entitled to abuse them.

PTSD flashbacks and paralyzing panic attacks are natural consequence of terrorized powerlessness. Blaming ourselves is the only control we have of an out-of-control world.

BACK IN ROCHESTER

Here's how the whispered story goes: Nona Addolorata, allowed to leave the state mental asylum for a Christmas visit, arrives at the curb of the house where six of her children did not survive, where her husband ruled and demanded she submit sexually to him every evening. Unable to step out of the car into her house on Christmas Eve, she is driven back to the asylum, where she dies years later. I am not told of her death.

Both of my grandmothers in state mental institutions are given shock treatments. More than once. Their whitened hair sticks straight up from their heads. They don't notice.

A cousin describes his boyhood Sunday afternoons waiting in the back of a sedan as his mother visits our Nona in an "insane asylum."

When his mother returns stiltedly to the car, the young boy looks up to the second-floor window. Dark eyes of our despairing Nona glare down at him.

MAKE IT INTO ART
Take your broken heart, make it into art.
⌐ *Carrie Fisher*

I am invited to present a full day on leadership and emotional intelligence on the other side of the country. Word is this invitation is an honor; the organization is well-respected and does important, nationally-recognized work. Our written contract is signed, travel arrangements are confirmed. On a whim, I ask my hosts, "On what floor will our session be?"

When the answer is the top floor of a high rise, I freeze. Heights trigger PTSD flashbacks. I have worked hard to face and overcome this phobia; but, a full day on the 25th floor would exhaust me and possibly plummet me into a debilitating panic attack. I level with my client that I have PTSD, asking if our session could be relocated to a lower floor.

Perturbed, she asks why I did not tell her I had PTSD before. Changing the room could be a major unanticipated expense. I collapse into myself with a shame attack and offer to pay the costs of rebooking for a lower floor in the building. I add bravely, "If we can't move, I'll present on the top floor and do my best," although I fear losing my mind, as I so often watched my mother lose hers.

I reflect on the challenge, calling on my understanding of the Americans with Disabilities Act. PTSD is a disability for which a reasonable accommodation must be made. My request for a lower floor is as legitimate as a diabetic requesting time to inject insulin, or a vision-impaired person's request for a larger script laptop. Shame about my "mental illness" has blocked me from asking for help. In addition, I am not required to disclose at hiring that I have a disability.

I speak again with my client, this time noting that I will pay for the room change because I had offered to; however, I suggest given the guarantees of the ADA, a change to a lower floor may be considered a reasonable accommodation so that I can perform the essential functions of my work.

The event is rescheduled for the second floor. The session flows beautifully. At the end of the day, I explain to participants why the venue was changed to a lower floor. I speak of my disability. I level without shame. An illness is an illness. I do not have to punish myself for having a disability.

ON THE PSYCH WARD

I am teaching 64 university students in Singapore, again on the top floor, this time of a polytechnic college. I am not comfortable with the height; however, I work hard to face it and talk myself through it. Classes are going well, but I am flattened by not being able to breathe. Driven to the emergency room, my limp self is placed in isolation as soon as my illness is diagnosed as a virus that kills children and addles seniors.

Doctors make their rounds, sometimes with interns. I tell them upfront I have PTSD and am likely not to respond well if anything is inserted into my mouth or down my throat. I ask for help in that case. I have established a cordial relationship with the head of the respiratory division, Dr. Hoe Nam Leong. He is happy to seek alternative approaches.

Later that day, a young woman who accompanied the doctor asks to speak with me. She tells me she has never heard a patient admit to having PTSD. She continues, "We have a psych ward for PTSD patients."

I get what she is suggesting and invite her to sit down. We talk honestly and substantively about medical and cultural views of PTSD. I invite her to tell me of her experience as a professional in Southeast Asia. I say I benefit from increasing openness about PTSD given emerging statistics on PTSD frequency in the United States. I add that I have learned to be an advocate for myself with this disability, despite feeling uncomfortable being stereotyped at times.

Later, when she leaves, I thank her for helping me understand how PTSD is viewed in Singapore. She thanks me for helping her feel more relaxed around PTSD survivors.

From both of these experiences, I am reminded of the stigmatization of mental illness. I am grateful to be alive when psych wards help people, rather than warehouse us away from society like lepers. I grow in empathy for my grandmothers and mother whose mental illness was taboo, shaming, forbidden and, therefore, unnamable.

We cannot heal what we cannot name. If mental illness is a natural organic response to unrelenting terrifying threats, our focus needs to shift to eliminating the threat to prevent the illness.

MEN AND INCEST

Now I can connect the symbiotic dynamics of men and incest, women and madness. With no place to be safe, threatened women "lose their minds." Being a non-person under constant threat is impossible to bear.

The United States Supreme Court declared "a man's home is his castle," allowing spousal rape until the close of the 20th century. Men, raised in misogynist privilege, can use their wives and daughters as they wish. There is no immediate visible consequence when the secret is kept.

SUGAR, SUGAR

At a cousin's wedding, we dance around the "sweet table" bursting with cannoli, anisette cookies, Italian pastries, sugar coated almonds, and chocolate dipped cookies, until the music stops. We are told to grab a sweet and eat it before the music begins.

This is a happy memory, this dancing and laughing. Being joyous and playful as a family is a memory I treasure. The sweetness of the memory is layered.

I sneak downstairs at night when I cannot sleep, a preteen in fear. Hungry, I open the plywood cupboard, locate and eat a small handful of Toll House semisweet chocolate chips. The chocolate soothes me. I eat more. My mother demands to know what happened to her supply. I have learned not just to pretend but to lie. My role models taught me well.

My sugar addiction, begun when baby formula was substantially sugar, kicks in and helps me escape into sugared oblivion.

Today, I am mindful of my addiction.

MY FATHER'S STASH

My father wraps his neck with a bath towel, dons his black and red striped belted smoking jacket, pulls a glass decanter from beneath the dining room cupboard, adds pungent liquid to his glass of orange juice and winks his secret to me.

"I feel another cold coming on."

TEETOTALER

My mother, a member of the Women's Christian Temperance Union, prohibits drinking in the house. Father disobeys with his secret stash, enmeshing me in his secret.

Mother drives me with her each time she represents the WCTU at daylong country fairs where she tends the booth illustrating the perils of drunken driving. She motions for fair-goers to sit behind the wheel of a car in a booth to witness the world spin out of control if the driver chooses to drink.

After I've seen this rendition once, I don't like to watch it. My mother is on her purpose, preaching about demon rum. I wander about the fair, noticing the hurdy-gurdy. When I find my way back to my mother's booth, the world is still spinning out of control.

Did I mention my grandfather was an alcoholic? Probably not. That too is a secret. My mother rigidly defended her father: "I never smelled alcohol on his breath." The man who abandoned his wife and eight children during the Great Depression has another master.

SEXUAL SHAMING

Preacher Earl Robertson's lecture is on the humble apple.

"If you don't like the apple's bottom, remember that part was necessary for the apple to be formed. It's where the blossom was fertilized."

My mother repeats this to me with relief.

"That dirty part of the apple is okay," she says with wonder. I note how her energy splashes around for a landing place. The reverend was absolving her of sexual shame from childhood.

My father tells me, "When we were first married, your mother would kneel at the bed saying her prayers so long, I had to pull her into bed."

OBSESSIVE COMPULSION

"Your mother has her rituals," my father tells me as I sit beside him hours after flying in for a visit. Lunch has been promised. I am hungry. "She's getting dressed," he says as if hours to dress are required.

At last I climb the stairs to find my naked-from-the-waist-down mother circling from closet door to open drawer, apparently looking for clean underwear. Her frantic eyes are obsessed. She does not notice me as I assure this bereft woman I will find clean underwear for her.

Her underwear drawer is uncharacteristically empty. All I can find to hand her are the least soiled panties from the bathroom hamper. She takes them and stops circling.

My father packs the car for a visit to relatives. Mother issues forth from the back door screaming, "Jim, don't pack the trunk like that."

She commands him to remove every piece of luggage while instructing him once again how to pack the trunk. Rearranging and screaming takes a long time. We are late, very late. I wait for the screaming to stop. Agoraphobia. My mother couldn't leave the house.

When we are finally in the car, she begins to rock and moan, moaning ever louder like a wounded elk from deep in her throat. She becomes nauseous. While our father stoically drives, we daughters urgently hunt a gas station bathroom where she can be sick. In the backseat, my sister and I do not look at one another.

This secret of hellish moaning must be kept. We wait as my father gasses up. Much later when mother emerges from the bathroom, she has regained something. She returns to her seat on the passenger side. My father drives on as if nothing has happened.

When she has these bouts with desperate moaning, bellowing, roaring in the dark night at home, we freeze into place. Invisible we must be. Doctor with black valise climbs to her bedroom, says something muffled, gives an injection perhaps, and assures my father she will stop moaning soon, retreats down the stairs, abandoning us to isolation in the dark night.

I come from a family of mental illness. No wonder I assumed I, too, would be mad. Without language or help for the complex PTSD from which I suffered, of course I felt I had inherited the curse of women and madness.

Today, I understand and am gentler with myself. I grieve for troubled women, exiled and hiding in their own houses.

#METOO

My 100-year-old father has fallen, taken by ambulance to a nursing home in Painted Post. My sister and I fly in alternately from separate coasts to tend to his needs. As I check in by phone, the head of nursing, after sharing her report, indicates she has something difficult to share. I assure her I am listening. She continues,

"Your father is touching us inappropriately. The first time he touched me, I thought it was accidental. The second time I realized it wasn't. I told him touching me there is inappropriate."

He responded, "I did something bad, didn't I?"

He hadn't stopped.

No one has said this out loud about my father's behavior toward women. I had kept silence for most of my life. The head of nursing is offering me her gift of truth.

I end the conversation there, thank her, affirm her and her staff in upholding boundaries with him. I arrange my next visit.

The next time I visit is the final time I see my father alive. His disdain for me rattles like a snake's tail. His distaste sizzles. I read the steely intention in his eyes. He is tipping toward the unspeakable.

I bring a scrapbook of pictures of him and his wife. Usually he turns the pages and shakes his head with approval or tsk-tsks his disapproval.

"Throw it in the drawer!" he snarls.

To relieve the intensity of his scorn, I ask who has visited.

His mood jumps the track from condescension to adoration when remarking on his granddaughter's recent visit, a highlight for him. Flaxen-haired eldest daughter of his golden girl eldest daughter. She is a lovely young lady, I agree.

I am used to these comparisons. I am used to his disdain. The force of his dark undertow of self-hatred projected on me unsteadies my knees.

He doesn't ask me questions. What of value to him could I say?

He commands I go with him into the bathroom.

My body freezes. I tell myself: *breathe.*

I tell him I will call a nurse.

I choose not to picture what he would demand from me in that confining space.

Wrath. His wrath sizzles like a hissing fuse.

I walk into the furnace of my rental car, parked now in the midday sun, blast my body with the AC's cold air and release my screams. Angry angry angry lonely wrenching from-the-toes-up screams.

I rage at our reality: my father will never, even in his last days, reconcile with me. He cannot surrender his need to abuse me.

A secret that could have killed me begins to loosen its grip on my soul. My father's sexual molestation of females is corroborated. I am not imagining what he did to me all those years.

I did see that, father.

Adoring baby girl, the one who looks like him,

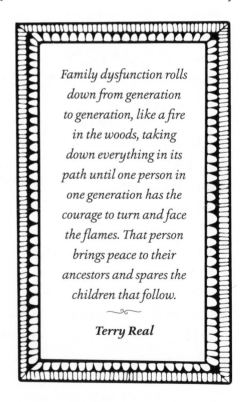

Family dysfunction rolls down from generation to generation, like a fire in the woods, taking down everything in its path until one person in one generation has the courage to turn and face the flames. That person brings peace to their ancestors and spares the children that follow.

Terry Real

strains toward her father. Adoring baby girl lifts up on her tippy toes, straining up for daddy's smile, hears instead, "You are dead to me, daughter."

When the time comes later that day to fill in my sister and brother-in-law on our father's condition, I alert her and her surgeon husband I need to share something difficult about our father.

My brother-in-law has already pronounced my father "a saintly man."

I disclose the Head of Nursing's factual accounting of our father's ignoring women's sexual boundaries.

My sister responds, "I've been worried we would be sued. I've seen him do this in stores."

Her words both floor me and stand me upright, shoulders back.

A secret that could have killed me dies in one POOF! My father's sexual molestation of females is corroborated. I am not imagining what he repeatedly did to me.

I did see that, father.

Secrets kill.

RELEASE

Our father returns to the house he built on Orchard Drive to die on an August morning.

Neither my sister nor I is with him. Hired caregivers sit with him night and day. My sister frets she is not there. I tell her, "He didn't want us there."

Caregivers report our laconic father talked non-stop.

At his wake, in his tweed jacket, hands atop one another on his chest, lips glued in a straight line, I kneel beside his coffin, rising to kiss his temple.

I release you, father.
I release myself.

I hold you accountable for what you did to me
and I release us both.

I take one final accounting of my father's continued absence, his unmoving face, his body soulless. My sister and her eldest daughter, kneeling at the coffin recite: *Holy Mary, mother of God, pray for us sinners now and at the hour of our death.*

When they take a breath, I say to myself and to my father, "God, grant me the serenity to accept the people I cannot change, the courage to change the one I can, and the wisdom to know that one is me."

I step back from my father's casket, turning to see Dr. Michael Gonta, my elementary school teacher, in his tweed jacket, walking through the door toward me. Michael Gonta was the first person in my young life to see me. I sought him out forty years later to thank him for changing my life. His family has taken me in; he is now my beloved mentor.

My heart weeps in gratitude: *I recall I am loved.*

CHOICES FOR HEALING
You can only go into the unknown when
you have made friends with yourself.
⌒ **Pema Chödrön**

Paradoxes, when the opposite of what I believe to be true is also true, abound in trauma recovery. I accept that dynamic without understanding it. Paradoxes include:

- Because I fail, I succeed
- Because I am so broken, I am whole
- Because I am intimate with sadness, my heart knows joy
- The more vulnerable I become, the stronger I am

Courage is required. A trauma survivor's courage is fierce. We value singularity of purpose because that clarity frees us from mucking about in the quicksand of shame. I am therefore enthusiastically open to breaking free, and work like a trouper to change what holds me back. Tell me about a way to heal from PTSD and you have my attention.

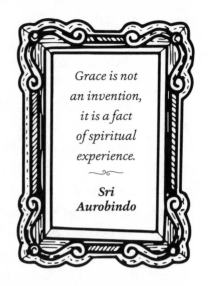

Grace is not an invention, it is a fact of spiritual experience.

Sri Aurobindo

To translate trauma's harsh legacy of despair into heartfelt healing, I choose, when I am able (I am not always able) to experience new treatments, research new theories, show up for emerging practices. The traditional "talking cure," sharing and learning from unlocking your story, works with a competent, compassionate therapist who does "his own work" to face his demons.

That and regular meetings with fellow travelers, Adult Children of Dysfunctional/Alcoholic Families, compose my baseline of healing. I have also with a professional's help practiced EMDR (Eye Movement Desensitization and Reprocessing) to redirect/reprogram my brain to accept, rather than run from, buried horrific memories. EMDR works well for many, moderately well for me.

Realizing I had no experience grieving, I stepped up to participate in Community Grief Rituals, in particular a ritual originating in Nigeria. There I learned to weep with and for others, to express my grief with my body, to allow myself to be soothed, to soothe, and to sing together a community's chant of healing. During these rituals, we bury an object imbued with feelings we choose to release.

I release a rock, thick and heavy as granite.

At last we share a family style meal, always with spontaneous laughter to help us transition back to our daily lives.

TRAUMA INSTITUTE, CHILD TRAUMA INSTITUTE

Paying attention to trauma survivors who admirably reclaim their souls, I ask them what helps. I follow up with research. That led me to invest a week of intense work at the Trauma Institute/Child Trauma Institute in Northampton, Massachusetts. Taking that risk required courage, stamina, trust and a significant financial outlay. Insurance does not always cover everyday citizens with PTSD. For full work days, with a counselor assigned just to me, I walked or crawled back into experiences I had long avoided in order to practice creative ways to use my adult skills to relieve that trauma.

We used a process called progressive counting, another method to defuse traumatic memories. After a day, I became confident translating the process to fit me. Thankfully on staff was a massage therapist who helped me release the bodily stress that accompanies buried memories. Each afternoon, I deliberately and slowly drove to my hotel across the Connecticut River and slept like a dog who had retrieved ungainly sticks from the lake all day.

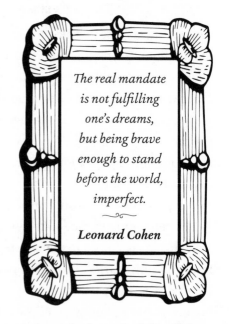

The real mandate is not fulfilling one's dreams, but being brave enough to stand before the world, imperfect.

Leonard Cohen

I did not run. When my brain strained to check out, I stayed and

I faced the demons. Or, I rested until I could begin again. This is, after all, a life and death choice.

SAFE HOUSE FOR SOULS

My counselor, Kym, as I told her of being beaten and my soul's escape in a point of light, mused, "The safe house for souls. I have read of cultures who believe souls find their way to safe houses with other souls who cannot otherwise survive the horrors of brutality. The belief is these souls stay in the safe house until they can safely return."

How soothing to hear this myth. My soul may have saved its sacred self and found its way back to its earthly home. How soothing like a balm in Gilead. Like the lullaby my mother did not know to sing. Like the blessing my father could not give.

Children stuffed in American border detention camps without soap, toothpaste, food, taken care of by older children, themselves suffering. Children sexually abused by caregivers. Foster children used as slaves. Japanese Americans in internment camps. Jewish families in concentration camps. My grandmothers in insane asylums; my mother hidden away on the second floor of our house. Political prisoners in asylums or prison camps. My survivor's grieving heart wants to believe souls can fly. To a safe house where they are not denigrated. Where they are honored. Where they are set free.

A fiction perhaps, but a soothing fiction. As another abuse survivor observes, "What's the harm in choosing to believe help is possible?"

HOPE IS THE THING WITH FEATHERS

Viktor Frankl in Auschwitz chose to believe his wife was alive in a different prison camp. He didn't know if she lived or if she had been killed by gas or other inhuman cruelties until liberation years later. Choosing hope kept Frankl alive and energized to help others.

During devastation, "always look for the helpers," Fred Rogers' mother told him. The helpers are the ones with perspective who see what needs to be done and do it. Frankl surveyed the despairing faces in the concentration camp and asked, "Why do some of us survive and others despair onto death?"

He determined survivors are the ones fueled by hope.

Freidl Dicker-Brandeis, imprisoned in Theresienstadt concentration camp, persuaded the Nazis to supply her with rudimentary art supplies so she could "take the children off their hands" by engaging children in creating art. Theresienstadt was the Nazi's "model" camp, used to persuade the world that atrocities were not happening.

Each one of Friedl Dicker-Brandeis's students died captive as did she. But they lived in those moments of creating art. They came to life imagining a world of beauty where kind people live. They painted their villages wondrous and green, not graying ash heaps of massacred bodies. The children sketched themselves relaxing on their backs in the softest of grass watching for animal shapes in the clouds.

KEEPING A NEW SCORE

My body has silently, like a loyal and loving dog, kept score of abuses and healing, healing and abuse for over seventy years. I now monthly treat my weary body to a PTSD massage by a gentle expert who works with military veterans and me. Quarterly, I lie back as my acupuncturist frees blocked energies in my body to circulate freely again. Water sluices to the Chemung River on its way to the sea.

These practices and more I experience to proclaim to Hollywog, "Sweet cassata-cake girl, I have got your back. You can rest from your hypervigilance. You can hug on soft Wilhelmina, you can swing out over the valley from the Old Oak Tree."

Hope is the thing with feathers
That perches in the soul
And sings the tune without the words
And never stops at all.
 ～ **Emily Dickinson**

Individual Reflection Questions

1. Have you kept someone else's secret to protect that person? Does keeping the secret protect you from the memory? What do you now believe about requiring family members to keep secrets?

2. As you look back on your life, can you now identify pivotal experiences and choices that led you to where you are today? Some of us zig-zag or wander our way through life, ending up where we were meant to be. Others of us set goals and follow them, ending up where we choose to be. Which describes you and your process?

3. Has anyone instructed you to put bad memories "behind you," "just forget about it," "let bygones be bygones," "get over it and move on"? Does that approach serve you well or cause you more trouble? Can you forget it, as they have advised? What might you do to set things right for yourself?

Book Group
Discussion Questions

1. Some people experience "the last great blessing" when a dying person, addled with dementia, regains clarity and speaks purely from love, making heartfelt final connection possible. Others of us do not experience that deathbed blessing. Have you found your time with a dying person to be profound in any way?

2. "In a disaster, always look for the helpers," Fred Rogers learned from his mother. What did Fred Rogers's mother mean and why would this have mattered so much to Fred Rogers, given the path he chose? Can you share an example when you could see helpers "around the edges," offering respite and care? Are you a helper at times like these?

3. What makes hope possible? Can a pessimistic person have hope? How does hope change people? What does Emily Dickinson's poem, "Hope Is the Thing with Feathers," mean to you?

PART 10

Tribal Drums Beat with Abandonment

A person's membership in his group—his tribe—is a large part of his identity.

~∽~

E.O. Wilson, *Sociobiologist*

Rejection by a group I valued felt like death. I did everything I could not to be excluded from groups that mattered to me. As the youngest child in my first-grade class, I wasn't automatically picked by other children for their teams. That hurt with an intensity I have only recently come to understand: being excluded by a group/tribe reactivates the pain of original abandonment, not having been wanted from early on.

I resolved to be popular because popular kids were not excluded. I figured I needed to be cheerful and outgoing to make friends. I decided to act happy even when I was sad and girded myself at age five literally to walk into the first day of my second-grade school year smiling and greeting every classmate by name. I pushed myself to excel at sports so I would be the first chosen for a team.

My strategy worked. I felt lighter, more powerful, safer. School, after all, had to serve as a sanctuary. I had to "keep up."

As a beginning high school "freshman" needing again to land in the safe inner circle of popular girls, I practiced every Corning Free Academy cheer to perfection to win a place on the cheerleading squad. Some of those cheers echoed the 1930's: "Boom-a-lacka, boom-a-lacka, bow-wow-wow. Twenty-three skidoo, wow-wow-wow!" That didn't matter to me. I worked hard to master them all.

When I tried out, I easily made the first cut; things were looking good! I felt accepted and hopeful. My parents found out and forbade me from entering the finalists' competition. "Cheerleaders ride on buses with football players and bad things happen," my mother carped. Mother had also axed one of my sister's desire to make the team by saying critically: "Cheerleaders' skirts are too short."

Why was I in agony, not being allowed into the inner circle? Fear of being abandoned plagued me. From my birth my father, disgusted with my having failed him, turned his back. My mother could/would not protect me from his disdain. I struggled to belong to his patriarchal family where I had no place. I gave up on being an insider in my mother's family because I could never be WASP looking. Although I learned early to create my own tribes of friends, I felt rejected by my birth tribe. Neuroscientific research reveals the "pain center" of our brain lighting up (becoming highly activated) not only when we are physically hurt, but also when we are rejected, humiliated, excluded and/or abandoned by others that matter to us.

"Sticks and stones may break my bones and names can break my heart" is more accurate than "names can never hurt me." Exclusion hurts, often unbearably. Bullied children commit suicide, desperate they will never belong.

Studies of the tribal nature of families makes this clear: To survive, we need like-valued people around us. We need to belong to feel safe. Not belonging is dangerous. We are hard-wired to fit in and to dread rejection. Hence, our fear of abandonment goes deep. Abandoned children are at severe risk of many kinds of death. Who protects the rejected child?

EMBLEMS AND ARCHETYPES OF ABANDONMENT

"You shall not cross my door again" my immigrant grandfather, Michele, told his daughter, "if you smoke." His daughter was nicotine-addicted. She smoked. When her father found her smoking, he disowned her. So goes the whispered family myth.

"You shall not cross my door again" signaled banishment from my *famiglia*. Adam and Eve were banished from paradise for eating an apple, the fruit of the tree of knowledge of good and evil. Adam and Eve had been warned: the consequence of disobedience is expulsion.

That threat of exclusion from paradise is devastating, elemental, archetypical, and common. Trauma is abandonment. Trauma exposes us to a dangerous situation alone without protection. Our brains store the memory as terror to protect us from getting close to a threat like that again. Even the smallest reminder can ignite our terror. We run for the hills to escape enduring the unbearable again.

Sociobiologist E. O. Wilson warns, "To be kept forcibly in solitude is to be kept in pain, and put on the road to madness."

One terrifying jostling by turbulence on a flight can produce fear of flying. One dog bite can lead to a lifetime terror of dogs. Human beings who have been traumatized will do anything to avoid being retraumatized. Our brains are programed to alert us and distance us from returning danger.

Being expelled from your tribe can make the expelled person cling to any family he has left. My friend David, a rabbi's son, chose to marry his high school sweetheart, a Catholic.

"You are dead to me," the rabbi father pronounced as he sat *shiva*, the ritual for the dead, for his only son. To this day, David is fiercely protective of his wife and grown children.

A lone wolf baying to the moon throatily moans human grief. Wolves cannot survive without their pack. Wolves hunt together and share their kill. Alone, a wolf has no help surrounding and taking down his prey. Hence, the lone wolf dies twice; once upon being shunned by the pack and again when starving to death or being eaten by a predator. The message is clear: to survive, fit into your pack; to suicide, be different enough to be banished.

The desperation of banishment is so chest-crunchingly painful that most of us choose to do what is required to belong. Security surrounds us when we are acceptable enough to be insiders.

Belonging, however, exacts costs. Punishment is meted out to those who do not fit. In gorilla bands (or "whoops") outliers are treated as inside-outsiders, scorned by the group. Inside-outsiders suffer the price of admission: *We will shun and mistreat you. You will be stigmatized as "less-than" all your days. You will be required to serve the band as the low status one, never safe.*

Membership requires sameness. Self-expression calls for different voices. The cost of membership is a slice of the member's freedom, the currency is self-hatred.

Did I sell my soul to belong because I was terrified of being rejected?

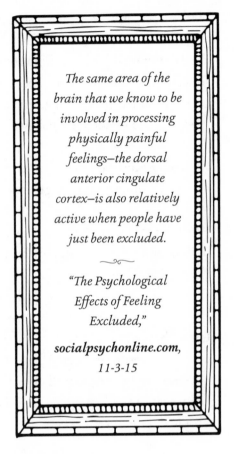

The same area of the brain that we know to be involved in processing physically painful feelings–the dorsal anterior cingulate cortex–is also relatively active when people have just been excluded.

"The Psychological Effects of Feeling Excluded,"

socialpsychonline.com, *11-3-15*

Every tribe has a (mostly unwritten) check list for exclusion. Each member of the tribe is taught from birth what behavior is acceptable and what triggers banishment. Every tribal member knows intuitively what it will take to be kicked out of her tribe.

Exclusion is so horrifying, folk suicide to avoid rejection's slow death. Bullies serve as tribal executioners. Bullies drive the abandoned to self-harm or annihilation Placate the bully to retain membership. Confront the bully to die in exile.

While teaching in Singapore, I asked my university students of varying ethnicities—Chinese, Malay, Indian, Indo-European—what behavior would be punishable by exile from their families. Expulsion was exacted on those who differed from the expected: the gender-fluid, the unmarried pregnant woman, the criminal, and sometimes, the mentally ill.

Reflect for a moment on behaviors that:

- Could cause you to be booted from your family
- Would offend you enough to exile people from your own family

We want to value differences. However, if those differences threaten family or group survival, people who differ are expendable. Messengers of change get shot.

HARD-WIRED STEPS TO EXCLUSION

Here's what neuroscience tells us about the progressive annihilation process that results from banishment. Annihilation splashes its harsh acid back on the tribe as well as on the exile. Exclusion exacts a cost both ways. The exile suffers physical death; the abandoners, having hardened their hearts, experience death of the soul.

THE PROCESS OF TRIBAL EXCLUSION

1. Two or more people gather and soon bond.

2. Bonding can be over anything and need not be meaningful. Liking the same sports team admits us to Red Sox Nation. Women who use the same nail salon bond. Churchgoers bond. Haters bond. As John Bradshaw said metaphorically, "Monopoly players meet monopoly players."

3. Once people bond, we begin to feel different from anyone not part of our "inside" group.

4. Insiders start to feel superior to those outside the group.

5. When the same facts are presented to insiders and outsiders, insiders will interpret the facts differently than outsiders. Facts and data do change inclusion-exclusion bias.

6. Insiders begin to shun outsiders, not to see them, making exclusion easier and desiccating compassion.

7. Tribes use "signaling," instant primarily non-verbal symbols/ clues as to who belongs. Signals are conveyed by baseball caps, ties, lettered jackets or hoodies, rings, tattoos, hairstyles, choice of transportation, secret handshakes, and anthems.

8. Insiders cease to view outsiders as humans.

9. This dehumanization of outsiders allows insiders to feel entitled to commit atrocities to outsiders.

10. The emotional consequence of being banished feels as horrific as being murdered. The consequence is madness, self-annihilation or "selling your soul" to be readmitted into the Tribe.

I do not consciously recall being excluded by my family from birth. Given my mother was in a psychotic and drugged state and my father was in a rage at me for not being his son, my birth was uncelebrated and worse, resented. Infants feel loved or rejected from birth. Mary Ainsworth's attachment studies confirm the consequences on a child's life if the child is flimsily at best attached to her mother.

In visceral pre-verbal, intrinsic memories, I likely felt abandoned when I was unwelcomed at birth. No one celebrated or was happy to see me. In other words, I was born with a "love deficit." Most traumatized children feel isolated with no one protecting them. Traumatized children and adults feel the "love deficit" daily when, no matter what they do, they remain banished from the inner circle.

My original family abandonment likely wired me to be supersensitive to future abandonment. After all, abandonment or "non-attachment" for an infant can lead to death. Hence, each time I was rejected, humiliated, shamed or beaten, my original terror of obliteration flamed, magnifying the intensity of the expulsion.

Psychologists call this phenomenon "conflation." The pain of one event evokes unresolved pain of a past similar event; the conflation, or combined implosion, of the two losses is unbearable. Pain is not only doubled: pain is squared.

For most of my life, I felt I could not exist without my family. Cost of admission was high: keeping deadly secrets, lying, swallowing shame and disdain, numbing my feelings while buckling from PTSD attacks, abandoning myself, accepting molestation and violence. However, I feared the costs of expulsion would be higher. I would have no tribe.

EXILE WITH THE COMFORTS OF HOME

I was exiled from my family during my twenties. My parents disowned me—would not associate with me or include me in family gatherings— because I was a "sinner." Unmarried women were not allowed to be sexual. I had made the choice to live with my boyfriend, Hank. For me that was a mature choice. I knew I was not able or willing to consider marriage, but I was committed to making our relationship a good one and I enjoyed being sexually alive. Hank and I, in fact, shared lovely years together until it was time for me to head north to law school.

Honestly, I was more relieved than grieved to be separate from my family. Being disowned freed me to make choices that were good for me and to continue my learning apace. Women's consciousness raising groups, circles of shared leadership where we told our truths about being women in the 1960s, became home. I made dear friends I could trust. We formed a feminist theater troupe, creating and performing a play about the Seneca Falls Women's Rights Convention of 1848 that produced the declaration of the rights of women. My role was Elizabeth Cady Stanton herself.

I experimented with new opportunities. Thanks to *Gourmet* magazine, I discovered I had a talent for baking, kneading my own yeasty loaves of whole grain breads. My supervisor at the university helped me find part-time research jobs to supplement my income as a teaching fellow in her department. I got my ears pierced, grew my hair long, sang along at fiddlers' conventions in the foothills of the Smoky Mountains, and strode down runways as a fashion model. Make-up and hair artists looped my long shiny hair into Princess Leah braided buns over my ears.

WUNC-TV, North Carolina's public television network, hired me to be one of two on-air personalities to research, write and host Thursday's Child, a series of eleven documentaries on school desegregation. For holidays, I gathered with Douglass LGBTQ alumnae friends who had purchased a large house together on a hilltop in northern New Jersey. One Christmas morning, journal in hand, I walked that mountain ridge alone, reflecting and writing about who I was and what I was discovering. In the 1960s, the personal was political. I began to participate in civil rights and anti-war marches.

I didn't know research about tribes then, but I knew I felt at home with my diverse groups of friends, and with Hank, both in my work and in my body. Had it not been for the occasional shame of panic attacks and flashbacks, my life was my own and I was grateful.

BACK TO THE TRIBE

My first year of law school, my sisters began to contact me to announce the birth of their daughters. I found I wanted to be a good aunt. In my final year of law school, I decided to reunite with my parents and invite them to my graduation. Probably because I was no longer "living in sin" and had put myself through law school, my parents resumed our relationship where it had left off, as if they had not banished me. We never discussed the rift.

When I married a year later, the family tribes came together into a raucous compilation of Sicilians, born-again WASP Baptists, and conservative Romanian Jews. I began my pretend life of being normal, acceptable, and dutiful. To none of these was I well suited, especially when suppressed memories of incest and abuse began to climb the cellar stairs to haunt me.

My family's tribes kept separate, meeting at funerals or weddings. Mixing Sicilian Catholics with born-again Baptists, dark ethnic immigrants with blond, fair-skinned WASPs, teetotalers with wine-drinkers, rarely worked. On my father's ninety-eighth and ninety-ninth birthday celebrations in Corning, I gathered both sides in one ballroom. People greeted one another cordially enough then seated themselves with "their own kind." Champagne was served for a toast. Ginger ale was available.

My father's funeral was the final inter-tribal gathering, as I knew it would be. Anyone who wanted to speak about my father was handed the microphone. Much was unshared and unsaid. Men spoke respectfully of the virtues of hard work and family first. Cannoli, driven in from Rochester, were devoured and bottles of Finger Lakes Riesling were continuously emptied by servers.

Vincenzo Bruno's funeral was indeed the final time these vastly different tribes would come together.

CHOSEN FAMIGLIA

My famiglia is chosen now, friends whom I value, can be vulnerable with, can ask for help. Holidays are often at my colorful condo. We greet one another, share a potluck meal and our stories. The room becomes magic.

My son comes home to enjoy his favorite home cooking. He savors the crunch of turkey skin and claims the turkey leg. On traditional mashed potatoes, he insists on pouring store-bought gravy. My gravy, a Julia Child concoction with wine, is not to his liking. Stuffing he adores; vegetables he does not. We joke with one another and reminisce.

I no longer hide behind the overstuffed chair in the living room at 12 Orchard Drive, squishing myself into invisibility to escape the blows, the screams, the belt, the disdain.

I no longer hide in plain sight either. I have too much joy in my days to fritter them away with dissociation, despite my expertise in that escape.

I am learning trust.

I am choosing not to run from love, either in love's giving or receiving. 'Tis receiving love that has been heretofore impossible. I relax my legs when they tense to run. I remind myself to open my heart to receive as well as to give.

Tribes can be wonderfully loving, even inclusive. I smile when I call to heart the faces of members of my biological tribes, for whom love is the blood that connects us. Tribes can also be toxic, assuming superiority and dominion over others both within and outside of the tribe. These dynamics are mutable; but change takes considerable effort.

I now understand why I as a four-year-old first grader felt insecure when not chosen early to be on a team. I didn't fit. I devoted the majority of my life trying to outrun the pain and danger of exclusion. In the end, I am learning tribes based in love do not exclude, they welcome.

Individual
Reflection Questions

—◦⟶—

1. What is your primary or "home" tribe? Are you in this tribe by choice or by birth or "marrying into" the tribe? If your tribe had a motto, what would that be? What are the unspoken rules of the tribe; that is, what are expectations for members? Are those expectations gender-coded/based in some ways? How do you feel about your tribe?

2. Have you witnessed the lone wolf phenomenon? Has anyone left a tribe to launch out on her own? How does the tribe treat the person who left? How does the person who left survive? What role do bullies play in tribes you know?

3. How do you explain the tendency of tribes to become exclusive to others? Does your tribe do this in any way? Can you think of examples where people outside a tribe are harmed because they do not belong to the inner circle or, worse, are viewed as "sub-human?"

Book Group
Discussion Questions

1. Why do people need to feel superior to others? What is going on within the person who feels or acts superior? What would it take for that person to change?

2. How does a tribe determine its leadership; who will make important decisions that affect members and the tribe as a group? How do tribes organize themselves to enforce the tribe's (usually unwritten) standards? What behaviors would get someone kicked out of a tribe, e.g. your tribe? How would the exclusion be enforced?

3. Neuroscientific research reveals tribes affect one another emotionally and have a grip on members' moods. Moods are catching in tribes. How have you seen this play out for better or for worse?

EPILOGUE
Mending the Broken Heart

The dark thought, the shame, the malice,
meet them at the door laughing and invite them in.
Be grateful for whatever comes,
because each has been sent as a guide from beyond.

Rumi

WELCOME THEM AT THE DOOR, LAUGHING

Thank you for allowing me to share my story with you. Telling the truth and no longer keeping secrets frees me to make sense out of otherwise unsettling and puzzling events. Hurt people hurt people because that is what they know. My desire is to harbor less hurt and to make more room for love. Truth be told, I want to translate trauma's harsh legacy into love.

My heart was broken repeatedly when I was a child. I received the message *we can't be happy and you can't be happy either*. I have discovered my heart can heal and my soul can be made whole again. Happiness walks beside me and is no longer breathlessly trying to find me.

I asked for help with my broken heart and I found help. Happiness knows my name.

BE STILL, MY HEART

In the ambulance to the emergency room, I befriended the EMTs with honesty.

"Listen, guys. Here's the truth: I have PTSD. If you have to put anything down my throat, warn me in advance. I have a killer gag response. I may push you away. If I do that, it's nothing personal!"

"You too?" They laughed with me.

"Afghanistan for me. That's where I got PTSD."

"Gulf War for me."

"Child abuse for me," I leveled.

My new buddies stayed with me in the hospital hallway, joking as they unloaded and rolled my gurney down the hallway. Other folk stopped by, drawn by our laughter.

PTSD, funny? Not at all. But the camaraderie of the afflicted?

Yes, that dark humor is shared in a heartbeat. Why not laugh? The alternative is despair.

When a curtain-boundaried room opened and my war buddies transferred me to a bed, I thanked them. Fist bump: We are all survivors, yes?

A tall, studious white-coated doctor with a rolling Greek accent entered, reading my clipboard. I welcomed him laughing.

"Hello doctor, I'm Holly Elissa Bruno. Can you tell me what's going on here? I was ready to be wheeled in for a colonoscopy and was delivered to the ER instead by ambulance. I'd like to just get the colonoscopy over with. I'm not going through that prep again for five years, trust me!"

"Your heart is in serious arrhythmia. This may be dangerous," doctor Dionyssios Robotis answered. "I'm going to try medication to see if and how quickly your heart responds."

"Okay, doctor. Then, we can do the colonoscopy?"

He smiled at me then, quickly grasping that humor lightens my load.

My heart welcomed those meds quickly and gleefully. The doctors required one overnight in the hospital for my heart to stabilize before declaring, "Yes, proceed with the colonoscopy."

First thing next morning I waved the queen's wave as I was rolled on my gurney down the hospital's hallway, happiest person on earth ever to be heading into a colonoscopy. You have to know how relieved I was.

NOT MEANT TO BE

Medication stabilized my heart for a while. Soon enough, the rhumba, samba, twist and macarena sashayed their way back into the chambers of my heart. I walked about for a sweaty week in August, encircled by the sticky tentacles of a heart monitor. The results were not great.

My cardiologist, Dr. Robotis, delivered my options.

"If you choose ablation surgery, you have a good chance of returning to a normal active life. Approximately 70 percent of ablations are successful; others never are."

Setting aside my terror of surgery, I made my decision.

Who would want to keep running out of breath and going hazy-dizzy? I had literally fallen off the stage at a conference hall in Austin, Texas, in a foggy moment without enough oxygen. I tired easily. My heart pounded on my ribs: let me out!

"How soon can you do the surgery?" I asked.

"End of October," he replied.

I was scheduled for 8:00 a.m., Halloween Day at the University of Massachusetts Medical Center's Cardiac Arrhythmia Center in Worcester.

BRING ON THE DEMONS

I had recently ended a 15-year relationship without bloodshed, in order to live alone. I had chosen to face my demons straight on, no longer self-medicating by focusing on someone else's well-being and avoiding mine. I was clear: I was not adept at co-creating mutually respectful relationships much as I wanted to do that. I had never grown up out of my family's unspoken terrors and dictates. Before/ if ever I would enter a romantic partnership again, I needed to let my lifelong demons enter the room to meet them face to face. Familiar PTSD terrors climbed all over me yelling:

Are you crazy?

You know you can't handle surgery.

You're terrified of going under the knife.

You can't even bear an anesthesiologist injecting you.

They will stuff a tube down your throat!

What if you wake up choking, that tube still in your throat?

You know you'd rather die than live in an endless panic attack.

You've never been able to handle anyone getting close to your throat.

They're going to shove a device up from your groin through your abdomen into your heart.

You know you can't stand men shoving anything into you.

You'll go crazy like your mother and bolt outside the hospital in your johnnie.

You can't do this. Tell the doctor you changed your mind.

Demons flooded up the cellar stairs to drown me.

What on earth could I do to prepare for surgery I didn't believe I could face?

I made a decision to tell the truth and ask for help. I promised myself I would talk, share, admit my terror.

I began by leveling with trusted friends:

I don't think I can do this.

I have PTSD. What if I have a flashback? A full-blown panic attack?

What if I can't bear for anyone to push tubes and instruments into me?

Friends, having heard my story, offered to accompany me to my pre-operative meetings at the hospital, drive me to the surgery, stay beside me after surgery, take me home, bring me food, especially the *pho* I craved. One friend drove hours with her therapy dogs from southern Connecticut.

MY TRUSTWORTHY TRAUMA THERAPIST

I had shared my story for the first time in its entirety with my therapist, a seasoned older man who listened deeply, did not judge, and was patient and soothing. When fear ambushed me as if often did or shame scattered me, as it often did, Dr. Gray did not run for cover.

Demons long assigned to the earthen basement scrambled up the stairs to devour my heart while it was still beating. Of course, surgery terrified me given my history, Dr. Gray assured me. He encouraged me to talk about what scared me.

Self-loathing descended from all the secrets I had kept about my terrors, my choking, feeling I was suffocating, needing to leave my body. I, at last, could admit that living like that was hell on earth.

> *Remember for just one minute of the day, it would be*
> *best to try looking upon yourself more as God does,*
> *for She knows your true royal nature.*
> *⌒ **Hafiz***

This secret abuse I had endured as an infant, a small child in a crib, a toddler banished from the table into a dark cold pantry, a preteen forced. Forced to massage her father's chest to save him from another heart attack. The preteen's hands forced down to his crotch. The teen beaten into oblivion. The choking suffocation of oral violations. All gushed out my throat as I told my story. Dr. Gray reminded me to breathe, expert as I was on holding my breath.

Do you believe yourself? asked Dr. Gray.

No, was my first response.

Yes, my heart spoke. *Yes, I believe myself.*

With those words began the long and steady, difficult and liberating path to the operating room and to this page.

I believe myself.

These secrets I have kept, even from myself:
I am an incest survivor.
I have complex PTSD from repeated childhood abuse.
I blamed myself.
I hated myself.
My mother was psychotic.
My family was steeped in deep dysfunction while appearing to be
the perfect family of highly achieving daughters.
My mother was wounded.
My father was damaged.
Both my grandmothers were institutionalized in "insane asylums."
At least one of my grandfathers acted like a pedophile with me.
My father was a pedophile. With me.
We are all terribly wounded.
No one is at fault. No one is to blame.
We are all trying to find our way home.

Dr. Gray and I met twice a week. He listened, at times wincing. When I dared at last to release the sound of my mother's soul-piercing moans, I almost plastered him to his brick office wall. His questions were rarely easy. I made a commitment to myself to trust this talking cure. I committed to facing and sharing the shaming things I least wanted to face. Truth, I chose to believe, would set me free.

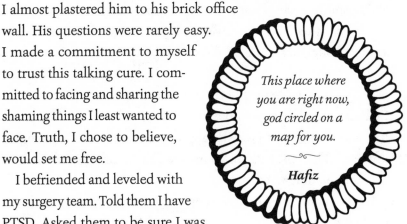

This place where you are right now, god circled on a map for you.

Hafiz

I befriended and leveled with my surgery team. Told them I have PTSD. Asked them to be sure I was "out" before they inserted tubes or instruments. We laughed together as I joked about my fear of running out of the hospital with my chic johnnie flapping about me.

As the days counted down, I became ready as I could be. I had told my secrets, owned my disability, PTSD and panic disorder, asked for and received help. I no longer felt alone.

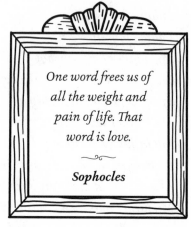

One word frees us of all the weight and pain of life. That word is love.

Sophocles

What had petrified me, in the end, liberated me.

I lay on my back for a four-hour ablation with a tube down my throat and a probe up my groin.

I did it. The demons too lay on their backs for a much-needed rest. I rested as friends took care of me, brought me food, streamed chamber music I loved, watched my favorite movies of the '30s and '40s.

Kathy and her therapy dogs drove hours to be with me. Those loving smiling beings wagged me to sleep, resting their gentle furry heads on my feet. Marina stayed by my side until she was sure I was strong enough to regain my sassy attitude.

OCTOBER 31ST SURGERY FAILED

I felt that immediately. In the ICU, my heart beat out of my chest. My medical team and I were disappointed. I landed in the 30 percent of failed ablations, with no guarantee future surgeries would have a better outcome.

I was not quitting. I had faced my biggest fear of going insane and made it through.

Let's schedule the next surgery were my first words to the cardiologist. We rescheduled for December 18.

I traveled to Sri Lanka first. Solo. I made friends, walked in and about bustling shops, bartering. I watched chestnut brown horses prance their riders down the Indian Ocean beach in the moonlight. I adored saris swirling reds, blaring oranges, neon yellows. I purchased jasmine perfume in a shop where I left my shoes at the entrance.

I engaged in the deepest of conversations with folk of many worlds. These conversations took place at the members' lounge on the eighteenth floor of our Hilton hotel. Heights had once triggered panic attacks. I had faced panic attacks and was getting better at preventing and diffusing them.

Treating myself to Shirodhara head massage, which I had discovered a year before in Kathmandu after my Chinese airline canceled my flight home, I was lulled by a warm gentle stream of healing oils poured onto my forehead, flowing through my hair. I emerged boneless.

From Colombo, Sri Lanka, I flew home to the arms of waiting friends. Did I mention that my flight to join a tour of Southern India was cancelled due to monsoon downpours submerging airplanes on the Chennai runway? I decided to enjoy my days wherever I landed.

I returned soon after to the University of Massachusetts Medical Center. I returned to lie on my back with a tube down my throat and a probing instrument up my groin. I returned laughing, welcoming my demons at the door, inviting them in, trusting them to be messengers with good news from beyond this time around.

My second ablation was a success. Dr. Robotis, celebrating with me, allowed that he had devoted an extra hour inside my heart to eliminate any remaining source of misfiring that would spike palpitations.

My broken heart had been healed from within.

ONE DAY TODAY

One day something will end my life as I know it on this earth. Today, nothing will hold me back from living in gratitude and awe.

Neither sadness nor loss, failing nor being excluded, not even a returning heart palpitation can rob me of my reclaimed birthright to joy. I claim that freedom for myself, my parents, my ancestors, my children, my chosen family and all fellow travelers on the path.

Happiness walks beside me now. Even when I lose my way, I trust happiness to run through the streets to me, tap me on my shoulder and whisper:

You found your way home, Hollywog, you are on your way home.

Individual Reflection Questions

1. Have you ever had to deal with something so threatening you didn't think you could survive? What happened and how did you face that challenge? Would you do anything differently today?

2. The author chose to disclose long kept secrets to her trauma counselor, and her PTSD diagnosis to her medical staff, friends and support groups. By naming her fears and asking for help, she found her way via the "talking cure." Would disclosure like that work for you? Or, do you prefer other paths to heal from your losses?

3. If you were to write your memoir, what dynamics/events would you find most moving to include? We all need to hear stories of everyday people facing impossible barriers and triumphing despite our human limitations. Did you believe the author would triumph given her trauma? What's one example of your triumphing over your own difficulties?

Book Group
Discussion Questions

1. Animals like the star-nosed mole, the crow, the snake, Wilhelmina the Saint Bernard, wolves, Timothy the cat, and Kathy's therapy dogs all touched the author's heart. Why are animals important to children, especially traumatized children? How did you react to the way the author was informed Wilhelmina had been killed? How would you share such heartbreaking news with a child?

2. The author faced trauma after trauma without an adult to guide her. Which of her choices as an "adult child" didn't serve her well? How would you have advised her differently if you had been a caring adult in her life? Which of her choices served her well? What would you say to the author if you met her?

3. Looking back at this book, what stands out most for you? What touched you most deeply? What do you take away from the experience of reading and reflecting on this book? If the author wrote a sequel, what would you want it to be about?

Bibliography

A. Tony. *The Laundry List: The ACOA (Adult Children of Alcoholics) Experience.* Boca Raton, Florida: Health Communications, 1991

ACA WSO. *Adult Children: Alcoholic/Dysfunctional Families.* Signal Hill, CA: ACA World Service Organization

Anda, Robert. Centers for Disease Control, Adverse Childhood Experiences Study (ACE Study), *cdc.gov*/ACES, 1997

Burke Harris, Nadine. "How Childhood Trauma Affects Health Across a Lifetime," *Tedtalks.com,* 2014

Burke Harris, Nadine. *The Deepest Well: Healing the Long-Term Effects of Childhood Adversity.* Boston, Massachusetts: HMH Books, 2018

Goleman, Daniel. *Emotional Intelligence: Why It Can Matter More than IQ.* New York, New York: Bantam Books, 1995

Herman, Judith. *Trauma and Recovery: The Aftermath of Violence-From Domestic Abuse to Political Terror.* New York, New York: Basic Books, 1992

Levine, Peter. *In an Unspoken Voice: How the Body Releases Trauma and Restores Goodness.* Berkeley, California: North Atlantic Books, 2010

Levine, Peter. *Trauma and Memory: Brain and Body in Search of a Living Past.* Berkeley, California: North Atlantic Books, 2015

van der Kolk, Bessel. *The Body Keeps the Score: Brain, Mind, and Body in the Healing of Trauma.* New York, New York: Penguin Random House, 2015

Wolynn, Mark. *It Didn't Start with You: How Inherited Family Trauma Shapes Who We Are and How to End the Cycle.* New York, New York: Penguin Random House, 2016

In Gratitude

The light in you calls out the light in me. When folk believe in me and my voice, Hollywog, that sassy child within dances, prances and skips over hilltops as she was born to do. To a traumatized child, being seen and heard is heaven.

Loving gratitude to each of you who believed in this book when I doubted: Sara, Tina, Nancy, Stacy, Kayley, Kaitlyn, John and the Exchange Press team for your courage in co-creating and publishing an out-of-the-ordinary book on an edgy topic. Artist Abigail who portrays light in darkness and darkness in light. Attorney Gina who assures legal boundaries are honored in this memoir. Janelle Brandon, my Virtual Assistant, who graciously eases every load.

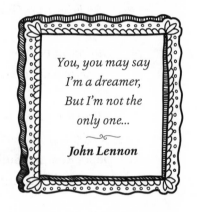

You, you may say I'm a dreamer, But I'm not the only one...

John Lennon

My tall proud lighthouses who dissipate the densest shame fog, Dr. Michael Gonta, William E. Severn elementary school teacher; Dr. Nelle Smither, Douglass College English Professor; Arthur B. LaFrance, Professor and colleague at University of Maine Law School; Joseph Brennan, Maine Attorney General and my boss; Gwen Morgan, Wheelock College visionary; and, my ever soulful Dr. Bernard Gray.

Fellow travelers who brave the path from hurting to healing to helping. Early childhood colleagues devoting their lives to making this world better for children. Caring, fun-loving, creative neighbors who make our 'hood a home. Wilhelmina, Tanner, Toby Grapelli, Growly, Leander, and every furry soul that heals us through unconditional love.

ALSO BY HOLLY ELISSA BRUNO

The Comfort of Little Things:
An Educators Guide to Second Chances

Leading on Purpose: Emotionally Intelligent
Early Childhood Administration

Learning from the Bumps in the Road:
Insights from Early Childhood Leaders,
with Debra Ren-Etta Sullivan, Janet Gonzalez-Mena,
and Luis Antonio Hernandez

Managing Legal Risks in Early Child Programs:
How to Prevent Flare-Ups from Becoming Lawsuits,
with Tom Copeland

What You Need to Lead an Early Childhood Program:
Emotional Intelligence in Practice